01895

# Fellowship for Today
# Lending Library

You are preparing a permanent record for our library,
so please print or write legibly.

Title: _PRIVATE MOMENTS, SECRET SELVES_

Author: _JEFFREY KOTTLER, Ph.D._

☒ book   ☐ audio cassette   ☐ videotape

☐ other (please specify): _____

This item is a:   ☒ gift   ☐ loan

PT

Given by: _KAREN BETTIN_
_____ (name)
on _03_ / _13_ / _00_
     (date)

# PRIVATE MOMENTS, SECRET SELVES

Also by the author:

*On Being a Therapist*
*The Imperfect Therapist: Learning from Failure in Therapeutic Practice* (with Diane Blau)
*Ethical and Legal Issues in Counseling and Psychotherapy* (with William Van Hoose)
*Introduction to Therapeutic Counseling* (with Robert Brown)
*Pragmatic Group Leadership*

# PRIVATE MOMENTS, SECRET SELVES

*Enriching Our Time Alone*

JEFFREY KOTTLER, Ph.D.

**JEREMY P. TARCHER, INC.**
Los Angeles

Library of Congress Cataloging in Publication Data

Kottler, Jeffrey A.
    Private moments, secret selves / Jeffrey A. Kottler.
      p.   cm.
    Bibliography: p. 222
    1. Solitude—Psychological aspects. 2. Human behavior.
  I. Title.
  BF637.S64K68   1989
  155.9—dc19
    ISBN 0-87477-493-4               89-30285
                                           CIP

Jeremy P. Tarcher, Inc.
5858 Wilshire Blvd., Suite 200
Los Angeles, CA 90036

Distributed by St. Martin's Press, New York

Manufactured in the United States of America
10  9  8  7  6  5  4  3  2  1
First Edition

To my brothers
Jim and Jon

# Contents

# *Acknowledgments*

A number of people were instrumental in the production of this book. I am especially indebted to Dr. Reed Larson, one of the foremost researchers on solitude, for his assistance in formulating the idea for this book. I wish to thank Jeremy Tarcher for his compassionate and constructive support throughout this project and Stephanie Bernstein for her editorial assistance. I am also grateful for the tolerance and understanding of Ellen and Cary Kottler in allowing me the time alone to think and write. Finally, I wish to thank the thousands of contributors to this project who wish to remain anonymous; their experiences form the basis for much of what will be found in the pages that follow.

# Introduction

$O$NE DAY I sat in the dentist's chair. Alone. Waiting for the hygienist to develop my X rays so that the doctor could check me over and give me a new toothbrush. Time dragged on. I grew bored counting the dots on the tiled ceiling and leafing through a two-year-old magazine. I found myself making faces at my reflection in the stainless-steel sink next to my chair. Fascinated by the distortions caused by the curves, I was just getting into some of my wildest facial contortions when in walked the hygienist. Caught in the act of portraying a madman, I smiled sheepishly. Of course, the woman had the decency to pretend she hadn't seen me leering into the bowl. But we both knew she had.

I felt as though I had committed some terrible crime, that I shouldn't have been doing what I was doing—entertaining myself with a few funny faces. It made me think how common such occurrences must be. After all, if I acted so playfully when I believed nobody else was around, what must everyone else be doing? Why do we feel embarrassed by such harmless and natural behavior? Many people talk to themselves, indulge in fantasies of power and wealth, examine their faces in the mirror for blemishes and defects, pray for help with their problems, clean house in the nude, eat with their fingers, engage in acts of physical pleasure—yet if someone catches us in these perfectly normal activities, we often feel embarrassment and remorse. What is it about solitary behaviors, including those universally practiced, that inspires discomfort or even shame? Why can we not even talk about the subject in public?

1

It was from such questions that my research into people's private moments and secret selves began. Over the next five years I studied the available literature as well as the intimate lives of more than a thousand people. Not surprisingly, I discovered that most of us could be considered quite strange in terms of what we do when we're alone. After all, in our private moments we are free to be our most natural selves. Indeed, almost one-third of our waking lifetime is spent beyond others' view—daydreaming, driving, walking, or simply vegetating, as well as visiting the bathroom, lying in bed, listening to music, and watching television. These experiences have meaning for us. These hidden parts of our lives are closer to the core of who we really are than the images we neatly project to the public world. They represent the naked self, unadorned by defenses and masks. It is while alone that we are completely free to indulge ourselves in any whim without fear of others' judgments.

It quickly became clear that being alone involves much more than engaging in personal routines and rituals that might seem odd, exotic, or silly to others. Our private moments are a rich source of inspiration, absorption, relaxation, insight, and creativity. It was while their creators were alone that all great books were written, great paintings produced, great ideas spawned.

My research took me far beyond recording the variety of private behaviors manifested in human experience. After examining the meaning solitude has for many people, I came to realize that the ability to enjoy being alone and to use one's solitude productively is not an attribute that should be reserved for the artistic or introverted. Nor was the need for time alone an indulgence—quite the contrary. The ability to enjoy and utilize one's solitude is a core psychological task, an essential tool for maintaining optimal mental health. People who find being alone a source of pain or something to be rigorously avoided are severely hampered in their ability to have satisfying relationships, engage in creative work, and develop a keen sense of who they are and where they are headed. Indeed, the whole spectrum of higher-order human needs—for belongingness, acceptance, approval, self-esteem, for stimulation and personal growth—is connected, in some way, to private life. Without productive time away from friends, family, and social and civic interactions, we can never recuperate from external pressures, replenish psychic energy, or reclaim our most authentic self. This became a book, therefore, not only about what people *do* when they're alone, but about the essence of *being* alone.

## BECOMING A MASTER OF SOLITUDE

*Private Moments, Secret Selves* is based on the idea that spending quality time in your own company is a skill that can be mastered. Just as you need certain skills and characteristics to interact rewardingly with others—openness, gregariousness, verbal fluency, friendliness, the ability and willingness to listen—you need certain attributes to be able to interact effectively with yourself.

This book was also born out of the need to bring the taboo subject of solitary behavior out from behind closed doors, so that you may be more accepting of yourself, feel less alone in your solitude, and realize there is a large community of people who think and act in similar ways. It was written to help you get rid of the guilt and anxiety that may be associated with your time alone, and to facilitate greater satisfaction with your private behavior. It is intended to help you feel more comfortable with your inner world.

The topics examined in these pages cover most uses of solitude—the positive and negative, the common and unusual. By being open to exploring the full range of experiences, you will increase your awareness of your secret self as well as learn how other people experience their aloneness.

With such understanding, you will be able to take greater responsibility for your own life and enrich the quality of how you spend your private moments. Most importantly, you will be on your way toward developing the qualities needed to increase your mastery of solitude. These include:

- Understanding and appreciating the significance of solitude and its place in your life.
- Learning to be more independent and self-sufficient, able to entertain yourself when social opportunities are not available.
- Developing the capacity to be more spontaneous and playful in your own company.
- Experiencing greater peace and tranquility after retreating from the stress of social demands and responsibility.
- Increasing your potential for creativity and productivity.
- Gaining greater access to the still, small voice within that provides counsel, insight, and inspiration.
- Becoming more proficient at counteracting loneliness, boredom, anxiety, and other difficult aspects of being alone.
- Finding it easier to love others after having developed the ability to replenish your own psychic and self-nurturing energy.
- Being able to teach your children to make better use of their time alone by setting a healthy example.

## HOW THE RESEARCH WAS CONDUCTED

You might justifiably wonder: How is it possible to gain access to people's most private lives? How can they be persuaded to describe what they do when they're alone—and be completely honest? Needless to say, face-to-face inter-

views on this subject are likely to be less than perfectly
frank. People are embarrassed, inhibited, and reluctant to
talk about their most private moments. Anonymous questionnaires have their limitations as well, since their brief
form makes it difficult to elicit much depth and detail.

On the other hand, observing people without their
knowledge or consent raises ethical problems. Such natu-
ralistic studies would give us the most accurate portrayals of
how people act when they believe nobody is watching, but
they violate the right to privacy. For example, researchers at
Brigham Young University covertly observed women in the
bathroom. Whereas 90 percent of the women washed their
hands after going to the bathroom when someone else was
visibly present, only 15 percent did so when they thought
they were alone.

While such studies are wonderfully revealing, they are
difficult to manage considering the insidious nature of clan-
destine observation. There is another equally challenging
problem in that these studies can only focus on observable
behavior and not the subjective private world within each
individual.

To work around these difficulties, I have relied upon
several sources for the voices you will hear throughout this
book. The majority are verbatim excerpts from anonymous
audio tapes submitted by several hundred people. With
their identities protected, people felt free to discuss their
most secret habits and behaviors. Other examples are
drawn from 1500 questionnaires I distributed to people in
various parts of the country, asking them to discuss anony-
mously their private moments and secret selves. I have also
taken extensive notes on my clients as well as students and
therapists I have supervised over the past dozen years, cataloging their solitary experiences.

While the people who were interviewed for this book
were not selected by random sampling, I believe they are
representative of the ways most people experience their

solitude. This is not a statistical study, however, but a descriptive one. I have examined intensively the lives of several hundred people in order to make generalizations. This type of research (described by social scientists as "phenomenological") is neither exhaustive nor comprehensive; rather, it is an effort to cover the subject of human aloneness by including examples representative of most people's experience.

## YOU ARE NOT ALONE IN YOUR PRIVATE MOMENTS

In the pages that follow you will find some of the experiences familiar and others quite surprising. As you hear people reporting what they do when nobody else is around, you may think to yourself, "That's no big deal," or, "Hey, I do that too." Other behaviors will trigger disbelief or laughter. You will ask yourself: "Can other people really be so uninhibited, so different than I am when they are by themselves?"

As you listen to people describe how they engage in their regular private activities—grooming themselves, working, creating, playing, meditating, relaxing, praying, exercising, fantasizing, talking to themselves, sneaking around, or simply doing nothing at all—try to view their solitary behaviors with at least the same degree of tolerance with which you view your own. You will be surprised to find a diversity of human behavior, and you will discover that you are most certainly not alone in the things you do during your private moments. Most important, you will find that with sufficient motivation and persistent practice, you can dramatically enrich the quality of your private moments.

# 1

# *The Significance of Private Lives*

ALONE AT LAST. As you sit with this book comfortably perched on your lap, imagine what it feels like to be temporarily cut off from the rest of the world. Ignore the other human sounds on the periphery of your awareness. If you are truly alone, notice whether you act differently when nobody is watching. Your concerns about how you look may vanish. You can slouch, scratch an itch, or simply stare off into space without worrying about how you might appear.

When you are invisible to others' scrutiny, it is natural to feel more relaxed. You are probably a different sort of person than the self you share with coworkers, friends, or even family. There are things you routinely do that no living soul has ever witnessed. Alone inside your own mind, you've entertained thoughts that would surprise the people who claim to know you best. You have a secret self that has been shielded from others as a protection against vulnerability, criticism, and rejection.

This private world is crucial to the development of a healthy sense of self in that it provides you with temporary freedom from social constraints and from others' approval. This secret self allows you to be selective in the demands to which you choose to respond. It contains the vital territory where you imagine, plan, and rehearse, where you fantasize and create, where you make those accommodations and adjustments that are required to keep you feeling tuned and balanced. Quite simply, you become more fully yourself,

unrestrained by others' expectations and by definitions of
what is considered appropriate. You are more uninhibited,
more expressive, and certainly more authentic.

## QUESTIONS TO ASK YOURSELF

It is a daunting task to explore private moments and secret
selves. Not only is it challenging to become aware of intimate things that you do unconsciously, it is difficult as well
to get other people to be honest in describing their solitary
activities. To assess the significance of your time alone, you
may find it helpful to consider some of the questions I asked
the participants in my research:

- When you are by yourself, completely alone and unobserved, how do you spend your time?
- How are you different from the public person most
  people know and love?
- What are some examples of things you do alone that
  you have never shared with anyone before?
- What are the obstacles you encounter that make
  being alone difficult?
- In what ways does solitude enhance your life?

As you take a few moments to think about your answers,
you may notice an interesting shift occur inside you. Perhaps your heart beats a little faster and your complexion
turns a shade redder. Some people report feeling defensive
immediately and close down their inquisitive nature; it is
just too threatening to think about private feelings and actions because of fears as to where they might lead. Yet you
notice another feeling welling up deep inside—a sense of
excitement and elation as you recall some of the magic moments spent in your own company.

You probably have a number of reactions to these questions. For example, many people feel an instant connection to the subject—a recognition that, yes, this is something they have always wanted to explore. This natural curiosity about how other people spend their private moments may lead you to examine your own private world. As Sigmund Freud and the Catholic Church discovered long ago, there is a direct relationship between the sharing of self and feeling relief afterwards. Another common reaction is the increased self-awareness that accompanies this introspective search. Most people have not really thought much about their private moments and secret selves because so much of the activity is mindless and automatic—singing in the shower, doodling on a piece of paper, or studying your reflection in the mirror are often taken for granted.

We are all distinctly different when nobody is watching. In perfect candor, none of us can deny that we act differently when we're alone. And most people feel uncomfortable about some aspect of their secret selves. This points to one of the paradoxes about solitude: the heights and depths of feeling that are reached, the joy and the shame. The particular way in which private moments are experienced depends on the individual's capacity to tolerate aloneness— a capacity that forms early in life and continues to develop over a lifetime.

## TOLERANCES FOR TIME ALONE

In a classic television advertisement, an automobile cuts away from a crowded thoroughfare and veers off onto a side road. The driver breathes a sigh of relief and smiles as he steers toward the vast emptiness ahead. Corny as it is, this sequence draws upon a basic truth: It is in the opportunity to break away from the pack that we have the best chance of

finding ourselves. It is in those special occasions of solitude—in the middle of a lake, on a mountaintop, or in the
privacy of your home—that you rediscover the thoughts and
feelings that most clearly define who you are.

Your solitary behaviors represent that part of yourself
that is so briefly and temporarily free of obligations and the
public image you present to the world. Although you may
devote much of this solitary time to accomplishing tasks
assigned to you or assumed by you to satisfy other people's
needs, you are nevertheless on your own to proceed in
whatever way you wish. A free hour or afternoon can be
used any way you like, whether for rest, entertainment,
stimulation, or self-discovery.

People vary in how they prefer to spend their time alone,
just as they differ in their preferences for how often their
solitary periods should occur and how long they should last.
Some people require relatively little solitude (less than a
few hours per week) in order to function effectively, while
others feel a tremendous need for several hours each day.
The amount and kind of aloneness you prefer depend on
several variables:

*The amount of physical space allocated to you in
your personal world.* A farmer who lives in a large, isolated house with only his wife, and who drives a tractor in a
field all day, is going to feel less need to find time alone
than an accountant who works in a congested city and who
commutes on a crowded subway from a small apartment full
of children to an office teeming with people.

*The quantity and quality of intimate relationships
you have created.* Those people who feel secure in their
friendships and love relationships, who have negotiated a
healthy balance of time together and apart, are going to
conduct their solitary activities at a more leisurely pace than

those who do not feel so satisfied. People who feel either smothered by their family and friends, or isolated and lonely much of the time, do not exhibit the same tranquility in their private moments.

*The early associations you developed with time spent alone.* To a certain extent, your parents' attitudes about solitude have influenced your own choices. People who grew up in households where solitude was treasured are bound to feel differently than those who grew up in environments where time alone was avoided or feared. Yet two children can grow up in the same family and be very different—one may model himself after what he saw at home, and the other react against such exposure. Birth order also plays a part. For example, an eldest child who learned to occupy herself in creative ways before her siblings arrived on the scene is going to feel differently about her private moments than a middle child who may have had more social diversions. The interesting thing is how relatively useless generalizations are about this phenomenon! That eldest child could now, as an adult, be quite adjusted to the idea of having spent lots of time in solitary play; or, on the other hand, may have developed an intense longing to make up for isolation she felt earlier in life.

*The resources available to you.* Certain economic and cultural opportunities influence your solitary preferences. Your social standing, cultural background, and especially financial and career security determine the amount of private time available, as well as the amount of private space you can enjoy. To be alone at home, it is often necessary to have ready access to property that is well secluded and a dwelling space large enough to grant each participant privacy. Wealth not only provides the space to enjoy solitude, but also buys the time to enjoy it.

*The development of your unique personality.* As you traveled through the playgrounds and classrooms of life, your genetic predisposition to be a certain way was molded and stimulated. You developed choices, values, and preferences based on the interaction of your personality with your experiences, especially those related to trusting others and being trusted by them in return, competing with others and feeling that you could hold your own, and reflecting upon the personal meaning your life held for you. Each of these tasks played a part in helping you to evolve a clear identity, sense of self-esteem, and fully integrated personality.

## THE RELEASE OF INHIBITIONS

Each of the factors mentioned above interacts with the others to create your individual need for time alone and your unique pattern of solitary behaviors throughout a lifetime. Similarly, your individual tolerances and tastes for time alone depend on other facets of your particular style, including the capacity for releasing inhibitions. Regardless of our individual differences, we all feel less restricted during private moments, as illustrated in the case of one professional woman at the midpoint of life.

Nancy juggles an active career with taking care of a busy household consisting of a husband and three children. The physical space in her home and office that is uniquely her own is minimal. She commands a respectable salary, but after putting away a set amount into her kids' college fund, very little money is left for her own use.

Nancy has solid relationships with her family and friends, who have no objection to her need for private time—as long as *their* needs don't suffer. She finds this conflict especially frustrating because, as an adolescent and young adult, she enjoyed a good deal of freedom to be by herself. She has the resources and the propensity to tolerate a high degree of

time alone, but because of obligations to her family and
career, she hasn't been able to make solitude as much of a
priority as she would like. As a result, she steals time alone
in short bursts.

"What I do with wild abandon when I'm alone is sing,"
Nancy says. "I've always wanted to be a singer. I have no
idea what my voice sounds like to other people, but it
sounds beautiful to me. There's something about music that
has always been able to touch me in the very depths of my
being. Over the years, when I'm at home by myself, which is
rare these days with three teenage kids, I take off my work
clothes. I put on one of my husband's shirts that is big and
baggy on me. No pants. My hair is just hanging loose. It
helps me to feel more reckless and out of character. I put on
a record—the choice always depends on my mood. I begin
by standing really still, as if I was in front of a microphone.
And I begin to sing with the music, revealing intense feelings within me.

"I start to move and dance, as if I were performing on
stage. It's funny, but I don't have any strong desire to be in
front of other people; it feels so special to do this just for
myself as an audience. That way I don't have to be concerned with how I look to others; I can focus instead on
what I feel inside."

Singing becomes a way for Nancy to release emotional
energy in the limited private moments available to her. She
is able to get in touch with her feelings and express parts of
her that she ordinarily keeps locked tight inside. The act of
singing is for her—as it is for many other people who belt
out a song in the shower, the car, or the woods—an expression of being alive.

Although you were most likely taught at an early age that
you should avoid doing things you're not good at, all rules
are suspended when you're alone. When you sing you hear
your voice making beautiful sounds. You can access the
memories associated with a particular melody; you relive

the past through connections between music and particular
sad or happy episodes. You entertain fantasies of a future in
which you perform on stage to an adoring audience.

As Nancy's story points out, you are less concerned with
your appearance when you are alone. It may not be unusual
for you to avoid makeup or shaving, or to walk around in
your underwear or with nothing on at all. You become less
preoccupied with posture and less concerned with how
things look to others—permitting a more natural and spontaneous manner of relaxation.

You are also less inhibited with respect to natural body
functions. All taboos and admonishments from society
are temporarily deferred during time alone; there is nobody around to enforce the rules or complain, "That's
disgusting!"

Solitude gives you plenty of opportunities to explore
your body, mind, and behavior. You tend to be more flexible
in scheduling your time, more likely to follow your body's
rhythms regarding sleep, eating, and exercise. You begin to
listen more to your own needs and be influenced less by the
needs of others. You are more ready to switch activities at
will—to drop one thing, pick up another, sit down, change
a TV channel, glance through a magazine, grab an apple,
walk to the window, wash out a glass. Everything is more
spontaneous and fluid as you are freed from critical
observation.

This release of inhibitions during time alone often continues to evolve throughout your lifetime. As you grow
older, as your interests and values change, as your economic
resources grow more scarce or plentiful, as you are exposed
to more books, films, and relationships, your private moments continue to change. They reflect what you consider to
be most important in your life, what gives your existence
greatest meaning and satisfaction. And yet the significance
that time alone has for each person depends, to a certain
extent, on how it is individually defined.

## DEFINING ALONENESS

Any operational description of what it means to be alone must encompass the physical context of aloneness and how it feels. These two dimensions work together in a way that at times seems almost paradoxical, since aloneness is both a state of circumstance (physical separation from others) and a state of mind (subjective perception of separation from others). Yet in all its forms and variations, aloneness involves a person in relation to him- or herself, his or her feelings of uniqueness and individuality.

The paradox can be seen in a few examples. Is a person alone if he is praying to God? While it seems clear that a person standing on an isolated mountaintop is alone, and one standing in a congested elevator is not, the sensations, thoughts, and feelings within each mind determine whether aloneness is truly experienced. If the person on the mountaintop happens to be a schizophrenic who hears voices of world leaders conversing with him about their plans for the future, is this gentleman really alone? The same could be said of a solitary four-year-old child conducting an animated conversation with a fantasy playmate.

On the other hand, place an autistic child, one who is completely trapped in a silent world, in a room full of children, and you will be struck by how alone this individual appears. You have probably felt alone when you attended gatherings in which you knew no one. All around you people were chatting, smiling, connecting, yet you remained isolated along the periphery—uncomfortable, self-conscious, and utterly "alone."

The way aloneness is defined depends on how a given experience is perceived and interpreted. To a large extent, this is shaped by the culture in which you live. Recall, for instance, how differently you experience being alone when in a foreign country or among members of a different ethnic group. Separated by language and culture, you feel even more alone when you are confronted by social behaviors that are beyond your comprehension. You feel utterly alone in a strange land.

## PRIVACY ACROSS CULTURES

To better understand the ways people of different cultures experience and define their aloneness, anthropologist Edward Hall developed the science of proxemics, the study of the use of private and public space. Following extensive research, Hall discovered radical divergences in how people of various nations treat intrusions into their private worlds.

The Germans, for instance, regard their private space as extensions of their egos. They zealously guard their private moments with sturdy structures built with maximum soundproofing, high fences, and optimal seclusion. German cars and houses are noted for the strength and tight fit of their doors. Aloneness is defined in terms of rigid physical parameters.

The English, on the other hand, are not accustomed to having space they can call their own, living as they do on a crowded island. They are more inclined to take refuge inside themselves. Whereas the German would flee behind a closed door when he wishes to be alone, the Englishman would mentally close himself off and retreat inside. In this case, aloneness is defined less by external circumstances than by internal isolation.

The Japanese and Mediterranean cultures, where physical privacy hardly exists because of the throngs of people competing for space, tend even more toward this internal dimension of solitude. In the Arab world there is no aloneness as we know it, no separation from family, no Arabic word for *privacy*. As Hall states, "Their way to be alone is to stop talking."

THE SIGNIFICANCE OF PRIVATE LIVES                                      17

Defining aloneness is obviously not a simple task. For the German or North American, solitude is a physical state characterized by separation from other people. Yet for the Korean, Iranian, or Japanese, solitude is much more an internal state that is induced by withdrawing inside oneself. Even across cultures, solitude is not only the experience of *being* alone, but also the sensation of *feeling* apart from others.

## SOLITUDE: FROM DESPAIR TO ECSTASY

We can define aloneness in terms of physical or experiential separation; we can also explore it in the context of how an individual responds to solitary experiences—whether as an intensely pleasurable and relaxing state, or as a tremendously painful experience of loneliness and alienation. There are those who are able to convert their time alone into creative energy, boundless play, and productive dreams. Others find in their aloneness a grim determination to seek some peace. It is the attitude a person brings to the experience that determines whether private moments become alienating or actualizing, whether they motivate productive reflection or destructive despair. This perception is shaped, in part, by the way one learns to occupy solitary time during early life.

Consider two people whose childhoods had a close resemblance. Although not without friends, both had a streak of independence that led them away from the group. They were both intelligent, though undistinguished in schoolwork. Both got along moderately well with their families, but both had much time to themselves. They spent a lot of time alone in their rooms, or in a back alley, or wrapped up in a book. One of these children grew up to be Albert Einstein, the revolutionizer of twentieth-century physics. The other grew up to be mass murderer Richard Speck.

What made the difference between these two solitary people? How can two similar childhoods produce such radically different adults? At least part of the difference lies in what each experienced in that time spent alone. For the young Einstein, solitude was consumed by his unyielding curiosity, vigorous inquiry, and an honesty of mind. For Speck, it was filled with loneliness and alienation.

After studying how some people experience their time alone, it was evident to me that distinctly different states are felt, even when external circumstances are strikingly similar. If these were plotted along a continuum, *solitude* would represent that state of self-possession when we are in touch with ourselves and temporarily unaffected by others' needs and wants. This kind of solitude sometimes liberates a burst of creativity and a feeling of perfect clarity and serenity, which explains why artists and writers work by themselves. It may also put us in touch with the spiritual or sensual side of existence.

According to scholar Oliver Morgan, solitude is a particular kind of aloneness that is distinct from other modes—loneliness, isolation, privacy, alienation, withdrawal, and even silence. Although a person in solitude may be in a state of stillness and quiet, solitude is characterized by *active* contemplation. It is a condition of attentiveness and presence in the moment that facilitates an emergence of integration and wholeness. Finally, Morgan explains, solitude is almost always a circumstance that is chosen: "Solitude is a way of being with oneself, of learning to endure oneself, of becoming comfortable with the mystery that is one's Self. Solitude is a decision to encounter one's inner Self, and only decision allows it to become part of one's lifestyle."

One of the characteristics that most distinguishes solitude from more negative forms of aloneness is the exercise of free choice, and this internal capacity can be developed with practice. Henry David Thoreau's two-year retreat to

Walden Pond is a beautiful example of how prolonged aloneness by choice becomes blissful solitude:

> I have a great deal of company in my house; especially in the morning, when nobody calls. Let me suggest a few comparisons, that some one may convey an idea of my situation. I am no more lonely than the loon in the pond that laughs so loud, or than Walden Pond itself. What company has that lonely lake, I pray? And yet it has not the blue devils, but the blue angels in it, in the azure tint of its waters. The sun is alone, except in thick weather, when there sometimes appear to be two, but one is a mock sun. God is alone—but the devil, he is far from being alone; he sees a great deal of company; he is legion. I am no more lonely than a single mullein or dandelion in a pasture, or a bean leaf, or sorrel, or horsefly, or a humble-bee. I am no more lonely than the Mill Brook, or a weathercock, or the north star, or the south wind, or an April shower, or a January thaw, or the first spider in a new house.

If such bliss represents one end of the aloneness continuum, then isolation resides at the other end. Those who are unwillingly abandoned, divorced, widowed, or separated from others against their will, hardly find their private moments to be the pleasant retreat that Thoreau so enjoyed. When aloneness is not chosen but thrust upon us by circumstances beyond our control, isolation often results. This is why solitary confinement is considered such a cruel punishment. To the Romans, the worst torture was not being thrown to the lions or stoned to death, but being banished, condemned to a life alone.

Yet between solitude and isolation are a myriad of other ways to be alone. Sometimes you can be alone and feel neither lonely nor exhilarated; most private moments are, in fact, rather routine, habitual acts—shaving, bathing, cleaning, or mindlessly driving. At other times, however, it is hard to pinpoint exactly what you're feeling when you're by yourself.

## THE NEW BIRTH OF SOLITUDE

The specific ways you feel about your private moments, and the ways you spend this time, are directly related to the quality of your life. The degree of satisfaction you feel about your solitary activities is connected to a number of other factors—the comfort you feel in your own company, the levels of intimacy you have in relationships, and the skills and propensity you have developed for entertaining yourself.

In addition, the ability to occupy yourself productively and contentedly will be one of the major coping skills you'll need in the future in order to enjoy life. Within the complexities of modern life it has become more necessary to maximize private moments because of the increasing amount of time spent alone. The work week is becoming progressively shorter; leisure time is increasing. There is a continuing rise in the divorce rate, yet life expectancy is increasing—which makes for more years alone after widowhood or divorce. Families, friends, and support systems are dismantled as people relocate more frequently because of career opportunities.

Now, more than ever, we see a greater tolerance of aloneness and a renewed urge for pursuing private moments. However, feelings of alienation and loneliness are not caused by the growing opportunities for solitude; they are the result of not knowing what to do with unstructured time. Our ancestors had no such problem, since they worked from dusk to dawn and then crawled into bed.

Because we have more time to do what we wish, many people feel some difficulty adapting to the freedom and self-responsibility that come with time alone. Your options for life satisfaction increase: you can do whatever you wish shielded from constant observation (and judgment) of others. You have the freedom to be utterly spontaneous, impulsive, and downright silly. You can relax when you want to relax, brood when you want to brood, dance when you want to dance. Private moments are the only times in which you are in total control of what you feel, think, and do, and if not, there is nobody else to blame.

Whether being alone produces feelings of boundless freedom, creativity, and joy, or loneliness, frustration, and anxiety, the experience is significant and meaningful for each person. With help from this book, you will be able to gain a better grasp of what your private behaviors mean, identify which ones you would like to change, and find greater peace in your own company.

CHAPTER

## 2

# *Appreciating Your Solitude*

$S$OLITUDE IS THE experience of being by your-
self without feeling alone. There are no sensations of loneliness, boredom, discomfort, or cravings for intimacy, since
there is full engagement with your self. You temporarily
retreat from the external world and immerse yourself in the
moment—feeling the warmth of the sun, the excitement of
a new idea, or the sight of a spectacular sunset.

Yet, enjoying a period of solitude does not necessarily
mean a rejection of the external world and a lapse into self-
indulgence. Imagine, for example, the voluntary retreat of
an artist who spends large amounts of time in her studio or
in the woods. Her behavior is hardly self-centered; rather,
the distance she sometimes places between herself and others allows her to see the world more clearly and to reproduce her visions on canvas. Through solitude she is able
to explore not only herself but her relationships with the
people and things around her. The same is true of a busy
public-relations executive who spends most of his time in
the company of colleagues, clients, friends, and family.
Periodically he escapes to a cabin in the mountains to unwind and reflect on life:

"After a few days off by myself I start to feel clear again.
My days at the cabin seem filled with things to do, but I
don't really *do* anything. I go for long walks. I plan meals
and do mindless chores. I think of places to visit, not because I want to go there, but because I want an excuse to
just drive on the curvy country roads. Most of all, I just
think about where I seem to be headed in the years that lie

22

ahead. I can't do that when I'm back in my normal life—
there are too many distractions."

For many people like this man, taking time out from
normal routine for periods of solitude is not a luxury; it is
as much a necessity as food, water, oxygen, and intimacy.
For reasons we may be unaware of or unable to explain, we
sometimes feel periodic urges to go off by ourselves, to find
both the space and the time to be alone.

## THE SEARCH FOR SOLITUDE

Every organism has a need for personal space, a distinct
distance between itself and other creatures. Ducks, for example, like to keep three body lengths apart. Cattle and
antelope space themselves uniformly across a meadow, as do
birds on a telephone line. Dogs mark their territory with
urine, threatening any invaders who dare to cross the scent
of their private space.

If you look around, you can observe this same phenomenon in the human need for territorial privacy. We reg-
ulate the distance between ourselves and others with doors,
fences, partitions, and other boundary markers. Envision a
crowded beach on which each inhabitant has carefully
marked off his or her private space with a towel and um-
brella; or a waiting room in which each person chooses a
seat that affords minimum visual and auditory contact with
others. In a classroom, we attempt to establish "ownership"
of a particular desk and feel upset if we discover someone
else sitting in *our* chair. Spreading out personal belongings
becomes a way of marking our boundaries.

Surrounding our bodies is an invisible barrier, a zone of
personal comfort that we do not want breached. Scientists
have measured the exact distances, nose to nose, that we
prefer to maintain between ourselves and others: men stand

24 inches apart while talking, and women allow 21 inches before they feel their space has been invaded. Total strangers generally stand up to 28 inches apart, while those who feel sexually attracted to each other close the distance to less than 20 inches. It may even be possible to measure how much people like you by how close to them they allow you to stand.

This need for personal space appears to be fairly universal. The very survival of any species is dependent on sufficient space for its members. When crowding becomes severe, animals such as deer, crabs, lemmings, owls, and muskrats inexplicably die off to provide more room for the survivors. Humans, just like rats, become unduly lethargic or aggressive when they are subjected to population density that allows no time and space to be alone. We can see this in the increase in alienation and senseless violence in our cities as they grow more congested.

Indeed, there is convincing evidence that the search for solitude is not a luxury but a biological need. Just as humans possess a herding instinct that keeps us close to others most of the time (as will be discussed in the next chapter), we also have a conflicting drive to seek out solitude. If the distance between ourselves and others becomes too great, we experience isolation and alienation, yet if the proximity to others becomes too close, we feel smothered and trapped.

Each of us has our own threshold of overdosing on social interaction and togetherness, times when we have had our fill of human contact—after a particularly hectic day at the office, a week of house guests, or increased socializing during the holidays. At such times we develop a deep longing to be alone. Maryalice Marshall, a psychologist and expert on solitude, recalls from her youth the incredible drive she felt periodically to go off by herself:

> In my mid-teens, I purposefully sought periods of solitude. I had favorite places to go, usually outdoors, which were con-

ducive to self-reflection and my ever-present search for life's meaning. One special setting was located in a large, private park within walking distance from my house. On top of the gentle slope, covered with trees and overlooking a small lake, existed a "natural" church. Several logs were spread around a majestic wooden cross. A totem pole stood behind the "pew," and a tiny log cabin was at the foot of the hill. This became a place of enchantment for me, a place where I could go to meet myself. I would sit or wander aimlessly, reflecting upon my hopes, dreams, struggles, and conflicts. I would leave feeling serene, replenished, and balanced.

Solitude helps invigorate our spirit and infuse ourselves with renewed energy and enthusiasm. It also helps us recover from the demands of social obligations. In an essay on privacy, Irene Borger describes her longing for time alone as a way to express herself more fully:

> During the months I was going around starving for privacy, I noticed I regularly enacted a tiny ritual. As soon as I got inside my front door, I'd kick off my shoes, get rid of my watch and public clothing as if I were tearing fire from my skin. The emotional cash would fly out from under the mattress, the skeletons in the closet would emerge and I'd find myself giving this great whale of a sigh. Gradually with enough backstage time, my hunger began to be appeased. Things which couldn't come out in public began to integrate inside me.

So strong is the hunger to obtain greater privacy in their lives that some people devote a significant amount of energy to securing more time and space alone. We look for the most secluded yet practical residence we can afford; its desirability is related to its remoteness, the thickness of its walls, the plenitude of trees and shrubs, the privacy of the backyard, and the height of the surrounding fence. Also important is an attached garage with automatic door opener so we can leave our private car and enter our personal domain without ever encountering an intrusion. Then, to

ensure further privacy, the house is divided so that each inhabitant has separate space. Each occupant has his or her own room as well as other private space—*her* study, *his* workshop, *her* kitchen, *his* playroom. Better yet, each individual has his or her own TV, radio, and telephone to further protect privacy.

Why do we expend so much energy and resources in order to satisfy the basic drive for private space and time? It is during private moments that we are able to build our levels of independence, inner strength, self-knowledge, and creativity. Solitude is the primary setting in which to promote growth and rejuvenation.

## THE FUNCTIONS OF SOLITUDE

In solitude you find a freedom of thought and movement that is not obtainable through any other means. Whereas loneliness includes much brooding over relationships that went wrong, solitude brings leisurely reflection about people who are important to you and an expanded vision of your past, present, and future. It is a time to contemplate every facet of your existence that offers either pleasure or confusion. It is thus an integral part of life that serves important purposes for both the individual and society.

Solitude allows you to fully appreciate all that is occurring within your mind and your life. Some theorists, such as psychologist Erich Fromm, believe the ability to enjoy time alone is a condition for being able to love others. Until you can become comfortable in your own company, you will never be able to love another out of desire rather than need. Dependent, destructive relationships result from both partners' fear of traveling through life alone. One woman explains how she worked through her need for dependency to the point where she can comfortably enjoy her own company:

"My marriage was completely parasitic. It reminded me of two creatures who, although they are bitter enemies, continue to feed off one another, sapping each other's strength, but unable to fend for themselves. As badly as I wanted to leave my husband, I was too afraid of being on my own. It's funny, but now that I so enjoy doing things on my own, I can't imagine why anyone would ever choose to be dependent on anyone else."

Like this woman, all of us have a strong urge to create boundaries of private space for appreciating time alone. Occasionally, as in the case of this woman who ended a codependent relationship to venture out on her own, many years of solitude are needed for the reforging of a more healthy identity. Most of the time, however, we need just a few minutes or hours to collect our thoughts and take a deep breath before we dive back into the complex, congested world of others.

In addition to promoting independence and resourcefulness, solitude serves several other important functions that make it possible for us to continue to prosper:

*Maintaining boundaries.* One of the greatest inventions, on a par with such things as the wheel, the compass, and movable type, is the door. Sociologist Barry Schwartz comments that the door is what creates boundaries between the self, personal property, and the intrusions of others; this explains why we view the trespasser or Peeping Tom with such outrage—how dare someone invade our territory without our consent!

Maintaining boundaries between the individual and others is considered so important that a good many of our laws are constructed to protect our personal space. And just as criminal law protects us from theft and bodily harm, civil law protects our psychological boundaries from libel, slander, and the infliction of emotional distress.

*Enabling personal growth.* A culture will not flourish unless its members are encouraged to grow. How could books be written, paintings be created, ideas and inventions be generated, unless people have the opportunity for solitude? The great majority of advances in knowledge and technology occurred not by committee but by individual initiative. A professor explains how time alone facilitates his creative process:

"The state pays me a salary not just to educate developing minds, not only to serve on tenure and academic quality committees, not only to advise students and go to faculty meetings, but most of all, *to think*. My primary job, for which I am supported, is to go off by myself and create new theories. To discover a new part of the world, it is necessary for me to get away from everything else . . . except myself."

One function of solitude is to provide an environment free of distractions so that you can discover what is inside of you. This may involve creative pursuits like formulating theories and sculpting works of art, or it can mean teasing out your own goals, values, and aspirations.

*Sparking rejuvenation.* Solitude also provides release of stress and the replenishment of psychic energy. Since it is not appropriate or acceptable for us to share our deepest feelings in public, we are forced to inhibit our natural impulses. Picture, for example, the subordinate smiling and nodding during his boss's tirade and then, once alone, screaming in exasperation.

Your time alone can serve as a safety valve for blowing off emotional steam. By learning to control behaviors that might be considered embarrassing, you save face at the same time the public is saved the annoyance of watching an unseemly display. Swearing, dramatic displays of anger, grief, defeat, or silliness, even various bodily sounds, are best done in private, where it is considered perfectly acceptable to let yourself go. This explains why you attempt to hide your face during moments of shame, tears, or anguish. Your own vulnerability is protected from others' view at the same time society is shielded from a destabilizing display of weakness or aggression. This is especially true in the case of grief reactions, such as the experience of a woman who isolated herself during her recovery from the death of a loved one:

"After my mother died I decided to go on a retreat to get away from everyone and everything. I went to this monastery for three days so I could be completely alone to sort out all my thoughts and feelings. I asked my husband not to call me and I told him I would not be calling him. It wasn't that I wouldn't be thinking about him, it's just that I wanted to know what it would really be like to be alone, especially after having just lost my mother.

"I've never lived alone or even been alone. I've always had roommates or a husband and child. So it was real interesting for me to spend these days in a room by myself. I literally didn't talk to anybody. I went for walks. And I just sort of listened to myself. For example, the first day I ate meals at regularly scheduled times. And then I asked myself: "Why am I eating if I'm not hungry?" So I started eating only when I felt hungry and sleeping only when I was tired. I felt myself slipping away from civilized life. And it felt wonderful!

"When I returned from my retreat I felt not only refreshed and spiritually invigorated—I felt I had come to terms with my mother's death. I was able to put her in perspective in my life. And I was able to get used to the idea that, without my mother around, I *am* more alone than I have ever been before. When you've had a mother your whole life, and then one moment you don't any longer, it takes some getting used to."

In our society the rituals surrounding burial and mourning are designed to make sure the survivors are rarely left alone, lest they think and feel too much and become overwhelmed by their pain. The moment a loved one dies, condolence calls begin as friends and family rally around for support. During wakes, funerals, and shivahs, the grieving have little privacy. People are constantly offering food, drink, and distracting conversation.

Yet, as this woman discovered in her retreat, solitude by choice—at the right time—offered her the opportunity to sort through what was in her heart and mind, to make sense of what had occurred, and to adjust to new realities. She did not wish to be distracted from her grief, nor did she especially want to entertain other people at a time when she needed to be by herself.

Private moments allow us to function in the social world without feeling smothered. When the pressure becomes too much, solitude allows us to withdraw temporarily in an effort to compose ourselves and regroup so that we may eventually rejoin the social stream from a more centered state.

## GEOGRAPHY OF PRIVATE MOMENTS

Your ability to appreciate your solitude is influenced greatly by the opportunities for privacy and physical seclusion that are available. Yet surprisingly, the places you can go to be alone are rather limited. By the same token, what you do when you are alone will depend on the unique characteristics of your setting—the familiar tranquility of your bedroom, the privacy of a bathroom, the mobility of a car, the congestion of the office, or the tranquility of Nature. The boundaries of a given space determine its relative privacy and, to a large extent, how comfortable you might feel engaging in a particular solitary activity there.

Jack Solomon, a cultural anthropologist and semiotician (a scientist who studies signs and symbols), points out many ways in which the personal environment dictates rules and regulations for acceptable conduct: "Think for a moment of what your home means to you. It's much more than a shelter, it's *your* territory, a private space whose boundaries mark the line where the rules for public behavior yield to those that govern at home."

There are things you do inside your home that you would never dream of doing in the outside world, particularly the many activities that involve bodily functions and care. The more private the space—that is, the more it has rigid boundaries that others respect and will not invade—the more likely you are to feel free to indulge your most personal habits. The more intimate the behavior (especially that about which you feel vulnerable), the more you require space that has been maximally designed to offer protection.

Even within the home, some spaces are more secure than others. The bedroom and bathroom are usually the safest environments for any personal activity. They are usually the only rooms that have locks on the doors, and they are usually the best insulated and most isolated spaces in the house.

## THE BEDROOM AS SANCTUARY

The bedroom is the site of a variety of solitary activities; it is, after all, the place in your home where you spend the most time. Your bedroom is your private sanctuary. It is where you keep your most personal possessions and where, during sleep, you are the most vulnerable. It is also a place for reading, watching TV, and talking on the phone, as well as for dressing, grooming, and other activities that are difficult to discuss in mixed company.

Several women in their mid- to late thirties, all mothers and deeply involved in civic or professional activities, spoke at length about their fondness for time alone in the bedroom when their children are occupied and their spouses are at work or out for the evening. A teacher describes her personal retreat:

"God, how I love my bed and my pillow and my comforter! I love it when my son is out playing with friends and I can sneak up to my bedroom to take a nap. I pull down all the shades so it's pitch-black. I unplug the phone. I turn on the hair dryer, which I keep beneath my bed for such purposes—the sound of it makes a white noise to block out all the other sounds of the house and outside. I just wrap myself up in the covers and drift off to sleep until I hear a pounding on the door and that beckoning back to consciousness: 'Mom-mie! Mom-mie, wake up! I want something to eat!' I try to ignore him as long as I can. Only when his voice gets a bit loud and hysterical do I eventually come out of my sanctuary, always a little resentful that my time alone has been interrupted."

In the bedroom you find the privacy for uninterrupted hours of rest, sleep, and the most private and secret of all human experiences—dreaming. Some of these images that dominate several hours of the night seem so real that it is as if the bedroom contains an alternative existence—one in which you can live a dozen lives in a single evening. Yet as exciting and private as dreams may be, each morning you regain consciousness and enter that "other" reality that begins in the bathroom.

## THE BATHROOM: SAFETY AND SECURITY

If you were to add up all the time you spend in the bathroom, it would equal three solid years of your life! You start every day standing on the tile floor staring at your bleary reflection in the mirror, brushing your teeth, studying your complexion, fixing your hair, putting on your "public" face before you start the day. You most likely end the day in a similar way.

The bathroom is a unique place for appreciating time alone in that you are truly blockaded from all intrusions. If there are any windows, they are covered or made of frosted glass. There is a lock on the door, and there may be a fan to obliterate all sound and scent. It is the perfect place to feel safe for any grooming, cleansing, or exploratory task that requires privacy.

Of course, this solitude may come only after some negotiation and conflict with others in the home, as one frustrated man explains:

"I think the only time I'm ever alone in my life is when I'm in the bathroom. Even then, I can't get much peace— what with everyone else wanting to get in. It must have been kind of nice in the good old days traipsing out to the outhouse. Even if it was cold out, you could at least get a little privacy."

Sociologists have studied this unique problem in modern life in which multiple inhabitants of the same dwelling compete for control of the limited bathroom space. Everyone rises at about the same time of day and struggles for occupation rights to privacy during morning rituals. Everyone in the house is fighting for the right to undisturbed peace to get ready to face the world. Like all habitual behaviors, bathroom routines keep life ordered and organized. You have enough to do in the morning without having to make a thousand little decisions over and over again. These habits keep things moving in a mindless yet efficient manner. And this is important since most households place a premium on private time in the bathroom. It is virtually the only place you can be certain you are unobserved.

## LIVING ALONE BY CHOICE

Some people are unwilling to negotiate with others for the freedom to be alone in the bathroom or the privacy to take a nap undisturbed. For such people, living alone is the ideal solution. Others find themselves alone as the result of circumstances: divorce, death of a spouse, marriage of a roommate. Whether one is alone by choice or by circumstances, solitude at home can be used for a number of productive purposes. For some—especially perhaps those who have been involuntarily condemned to aloneness by death, divorce, rejection, or withdrawal—living alone can be difficult. Some find it stressful, boring, and lonely. But with sufficient practice and motivation, solitary living can become quite comfortable.

In a book for women who feel helpless, angry, and frustrated without a partner, and depressed and lonely with themselves as a companion, author Penelope Russianoff suggests that a change in attitude might make a difference:

> Living alone is just like being married—except the relationship you are having is with yourself. Like marriage, living alone has its ups and downs. Sometimes you hate yourself, and sometimes you love yourself; sometimes you're at odds with yourself. There are days you find yourself fascinating and days you find yourself an intolerable pain in the ass. And here is where my little analogy falls apart. Because one thing you can't do alone, as in marriage, is to stalk into the other room and slam the door in your face.

When you are alone, there is nobody else to blame if things are not the way you would like them to be. You are forced to assume more control over your life, more responsibility for the directions it is taking.

People who like living alone report a special appreciation for quiet and relaxation. They enjoy the restful solitude of reading the paper with their feet propped on the table. No intrusions, no distractions, nobody crying for attention. They feel a sense of pride in solitary ownership, knowing that who they are and what they have is the result of their own labors. They thus develop greater inner resources and feel satisfaction in their independence and ability to take care of themselves. People who live alone enjoy greater privacy to be thoroughly themselves. They feel more natural and act with fewer inhibitions.

Those who don't live alone can learn a lot from those who do, especially with regard to taking care of one's own needs and listening to one's own rhythms. It is not necessary to live alone to feel free. As will be discussed in a later chapter, in a respectful, open, caring relationship or family structure it is possible to negotiate time for solitude without sacrificing the quality of other relationships. For a surprising number of people, however, solitude is a precious commodity indeed—in some cases, limited to fleeting moments of solitary travel in an automobile.

## THE CAR: FRONTIER OF PRIVACY

In their book *Driving Passion: The Psychology of the Car,* Peter Marsh and Peter Collett explore the reasons why we are obsessed with our cars. Cars supply us with a womblike security reminiscent of a living room, complete with comfortable lounge chairs, entertainment centers, and spacious windows. We feel invulnerable and untouchable when surrounded by this speeding object, which by its very appearance makes a statement about how we see ourselves and how we want others to see us. The authors explain the transformation that often takes place when we reveal our secret selves inside an automobile:

> When people get behind the wheel of a car they become seemingly stronger and more powerful. Completely new opportunities arise for mastery, enclosed within a private space that shields the driver from the concerns that ordinarily beset his or her life. People report a sense of freedom, a condition where they can shut out negative experiences and simultaneously admit new pleasures. The only contact with the world is through the vibrations of the steering wheel and

the sight of the landscape rushing past—a psychological experience of detachment, but also of special involvement.

The automobile has been the last frontier of personal privacy. However, since the advent of the car phone, this sacred solitude is rapidly dwindling. No longer can you expect to escape the pressures and demands of home and office as you drive along. One moment you are off inside your own world, cruising down the road, and the next moment the ringing phone brings you back to the land of obligations. Some people even take their portable phones to the golf course, to concerts, or on walks, concerned they might miss that one important call. The price they pay for this permanent umbilical cord to the fast lane of life, of course, is greater stress and considerably less tranquil solitude. Perhaps one day we'll all wear little phones like waterproof wristwatches, carrying on conversations in the shower. Solitude, as we now know it, could someday end.

One consultant who travels a lot refuses to give in to pressure from his colleagues to install a telephone in his car because he much prefers to talk to himself when driving:

"I can't imagine having a phone in my car. One of the things I love about driving is that the car is the one place I can escape from other people who want something from me. I sit perched on my seat traveling seventy-five miles per hour down the highway, watching the scenery flow by, a landscape that is forever changing. I love to sing along with the radio. And I love to talk to myself. If I ever feel the urge to talk to somebody else on one of my long trips, I like to make tapes on a recorder I carry with me. I conduct these long monologues. I feel so uninhibited talking to someone who is not really there. I can easily fill up a ninety-minute tape just chattering away about what is going on in my head or my life. My friends so appreciate getting these tapes in the mail because they are so honest and spontaneous."

Barring car phones, the automobile is a place where we

can be totally protected from outside intrusions. In fact, we are so protective of our private space that we tend to over-react if somebody else's car gets too close. We honk the horn in indignation and drive aggressively if we believe our territory has been infringed upon. Even the most mild-mannered people will draw the line when in a car. In the words of one woman:

"I don't know what gets into me when I'm driving. It feels like the one place in life that I'm safe. I know that sounds crazy considering all the ways there are to be killed on the highway, but when I'm in my car by myself it feels like nothing can get to me and nobody can yell at me. It's just me and the radio and the steering wheel. It's such freedom to be able to go wherever I want. I don't know why I get so upset when somebody cuts me off, but I just go nuts. I swear like you wouldn't believe, and in the only area of my life, I scream back at somebody else."

It is easy to become carried away with the illusion of complete privacy in the car, because we are alone in the sense that nobody can hear us or get to us in our moving capsule. But we tend to forget we are in plain view of others. One woman remarks on this phenomenon:

"I remember once I was repositioning my bra when I happened to look over and see this guy in a van staring at me. I just pretended like nothing happened, hoping he would think he had been hallucinating. Thank God I had a faster car so I could take off out of there!"

In spite of the visibility a car affords, it still provides sufficient privacy to engage in a number of solitary activities, from daydreaming to the most common car activity of all—listening to the radio. One woman, who says it seems she spends half her life stuck on congested freeways, combines the use of fantasy and radio into a wonderful form of solitary entertainment:

"During the sixties, when everyone else was being a 'flower child,' I was married and had a few kids. I always wanted to be a hippie, to wear bell-bottoms, let my hair grow long, smoke dope all night, and go to peace marches during the day. But I had responsibilities I couldn't ignore, so I watched enviously as others had fun.

"When I get in the car I listen to only sixties music on the radio. There are a few stations that play the Beatles, Rolling Stones, Janis Joplin, and Jimi Hendrix all day. I drive along and slip back into the past when this music was popular. And I imagine myself as a 'flower child' without a care in the world. It's such a contrast with what happens when I turn off the ignition and step outside my car into the hectic world that is waiting for me."

## PERSONAL SPACE AND TIME AT THE OFFICE

Since many people spend more time at work than at home, the office is a second residence, but one with less privacy. Nevertheless, each office worker has a sense of personal private space, even if it is demarcated by nothing more than a plant, a partition, or family photographs on a desk. Even those whose only personal territory at work is a small cubicle or desk are able to indulge themselves in solitary activites that are not work-related. In fact, we spend a significant part of our work day alone, taking care of solitary business—getting coffee, making trips to the bathroom, finding a private corner to adjust an article of clothing, fantasizing, reading the paper, doodling on a pad, freshening makeup, playing video games on the computer, or just staring off into space.

The most effective way to insure private time and space at the office is to be the first to arrive. One woman so enjoys this quiet time that she makes a point of getting an early start:

"At my office, I'm the first one to open things up, so I usually heat up the water for tea. It takes two minutes. So what do I do for two minutes? Should I go back to my office or wait for it? Well, I like to sing, and I used to be in a choir. So what I do is hum with the microwave. First, I turn the thing on, and as it warms up I listen closely to its pitch. Then I harmonize and sing with it. The microwave and I play together—at least until I hear the sounds of other people arriving for work."

After the strenuous concentration required during work-related activities, and after endless interactions on the phone or in meetings, it is often necessary to steal time alone for recovery and rejuvenation. A psychologist describes what he does with his time between scheduled appointments:

"When I need a boost during the day, I listen to music through headphones to pick myself up. Ever since I read that lions and other mammals take naps in the late afternoon, and that most industrial accidents take place between three and four P.M., I've noticed how my own biorhythms take a dive at that time. I try not to schedule three o'clock appointments because I yawn the whole session. But when I do, I spend a few minutes after the previous session with the headphones on. Sometimes I do stretching exercises to the beat. It seems to make a difference in getting my creative juices flowing for my next session."

An advertising writer who works in a high-pressure environment, describes the way she relaxes in the office between assignments:

"I'm paid to think up ideas. Most of my time I'm sequestered away in my office. Since there are windows all around me, people can see what I'm up to, so I have to look busy. I don't know what someone who is busy thinking is supposed to look like, but I know my group head would get upset if she saw me doing my nails or something. That's too bad, because I've had some great ideas while I do my nails.

"I think I feel more professional with a pen in my hand and a pad of paper in front of me. The thing is that writing down notes doesn't help me much. I like to free associate. So what I write down on the paper are just meaningless doodles. It reminds me of algebra class where I'd sit there writing my name next to a boy's name who I was in love with at the time. I'd draw boy's faces or body parts, or just practice signing my name in different styles. Now that I'm older I don't do that stuff anymore. Oh, I still draw boy's body parts, but I'm sure my doodles are more mature. So there I sit in my glass cubicle staring off into space thinking about a new laundry soap or limousine service, pen in hand, doodling all day. I hope my boss never checks my wastebasket."

Those who work for themselves, or whose work takes them away from others' scrutiny, have even more flexibility in how they use private moments to escape from daily routine. One such person is a sculptor who works in a gigantic warehouse. What he does to break up his routine reflects his high energy level. He has less of a need to relax between periods of concentration than he does to simply change his moods:

"In my studio I put on roller skates a lot. I put on some loud music and skate all around the warehouse. I usually have about five projects going at the same time—maybe three art projects and, in between, cleaning up the place, cooking some lunch. I skate from one of these stations to the next. I might work on a sculpture, casting something, and then while I wait for it to dry, I skate over to the refrigerator and grab a beer. Then I skate over to another piece to do some welding (not an easy task on roller skates). Then I skate over to my saxophone and play a few tunes as I weave in and out between my work tables. Then something catches my eye, so I stop and diddle a bit with a water sculpture I'm creating. Then back over to the kitchen for something to eat. That's great fun, dancing, working, having a good old time."

The exuberance and spontaneity of this young man's

narrative exemplify the freedom of self-expression that is possible during time alone. Regardless of the particular geographical space you find yourself in, whether at home, at work, or anywhere in between, your private life reflects your innermost needs and your heartfelt desires. This time alone is virtually a requirement in order for you to develop a sense of individual identity. For whether you are barricaded in the bathroom, or have retreated inside yourself while in a crowd, your feelings, thoughts, and unique ideas are formed during your private moments.

## THE FREEDOM OF NATURE

The type of mental solitude you can achieve is enhanced when you are out in Nature. There your inner solitude is matched by an external aloneness. You have no one to be concerned about but yourself, no voices to listen to but your own. One reason people seek solitude in the outdoors is to immerse themselves in the most natural of all environments. In Nature, you are free of all human intrusions. No telephone, no television, no neighbors, no noise. Just the sounds and sights of the wilderness.

Liberated from external demands and schedules, you are free to focus your attention wherever you like. You can choose any direction to think, to walk, to explore. You can dress however you like (the trees and birds don't care). You can eat when you feel like it, wash if you want to, and generally follow the body's natural rhythms.

When unobserved in the sanctuary of Nature you are free to literally let yourself go. Such privacy enables you to indulge in various postures you would be embarrassed to display in public. Reverting to these more natural states allows you to feel more free, comfortable, and accepting of yourself—without makeup or a public mask.

Certain commands from childhood come back to haunt

us: "Don't slouch!" "Keep your legs together, young lady!" "If you don't stop making that expression, your face might freeze." "Cover your mouth!"

The effect of these admonitions is a body held rigid and a demeanor that is controlled. Under such conditions, during your waking hours your authentic self becomes buried. It is only during time alone that you are able to relax completely. Sometimes, the more natural the environment, the easier it is to revert to a more tranquil state. Under these conditions, in the woods or wherever you feel most natural and unobserved, you will find it easier to do any of the following:

- to consider aspects of your life that are in need of attention
- to relive experiences from the past that bring you pleasure or learning
- to plan the future—where you are headed and how you intend to get there
- to be more aware of your unfulfilled desires
- to enjoy tranquility and self-renewal
- to seek adventure and take risks that can only be accomplished alone

We have examined why there is such a strong desire for solitude, some of the functions solitude serves for the individual and society, and how private behavior is influenced by the geographic context in which it takes place. Let's look more closely at the reasons why some people search out solitude, and in so doing, risk facing the unknown.

## THE PURSUIT OF PEAK EXPERIENCES

According to Abraham Maslow, a pioneer of humanistic psychology, one of the characteristics of self-actualized people is a high frequency of "peak experiences," or private moments that are filled with rapture. Among the qualities noted by Maslow in people who are psychologically healthy are:

- acceptance of self and others
- autonomy and independence
- creative and spontaneous nature
- satisfying interpersonal relationships
- superior perception of reality
- richness of emotional responses
- skill in problem solving
- growth orientation to life
- openness to new experiences
- intense desire for solitude
- high frequency of peak experiences

The last two qualities are of particular interest. According to Maslow and many other experts on mental health, the most well-adjusted individuals are those who are able to seek out and enjoy their time alone. They are able to experience peak moments of joy on a consistent basis, especially when they are in their own company.

One social-science teacher, like many of his colleagues, looks forward to his summer vacations as a break from his usual routines. Jay sees his professional role as geared not so much toward imparting any specific information to his students as to presenting himself as a model of an adult who is reasonably well adjusted. In fact, he is one of the most popular teachers in his school because of his spontaneity, enthusiasm, genuine caring, and rock-solid stability. He uses his summer vacations to decompress from the year's pressures and rediscover his inner world. One summer he took a solo cross-country trip by motorcycle; another year he bicycled around the Great Lakes. Recently he took a month by himself to wander through Europe:

"It is such a great feeling to be completely free of schedules and programmed days. On any given morning I can hop on a train going in any direction that strikes my fancy. One day I started hitchhiking toward Italy, and after three hours of watching cars pass me by, I crossed to the other side of the road and immediately found a ride to Denmark.

"Among the most significant experiences of my life is hiking in the mountains. I recall one instance of being in the Alps. I walked up trails through trees, rocky cliffs, and meadows gleaming with flowers in yellow, white, and purple. The snowy peaks rise in the distance. I don't think I've ever heard such total quiet. The only sounds were of my labored breathing and the wind blowing through the trees. After a while I would start to hum to myself, just to hear a sound. But the most amazing thing is how my brain shuts down. You have to understand I am *always* thinking about stuff. But once in that atmosphere, I just seem to lose myself in what I'm experiencing. The whole afternoon I can't recall a single conscious thought except: 'Maybe I can step here.' 'Will this rock hold?' Or, 'Wow, look at that!'"

The solitary peak experience Jay describes is an example of what is possible when you are fully absorbed in the present moment. Perception is heightened, as is emotional receptivity. You feel a disorientation in time and space, a sense that life is happening outside ordinary reality. For Jay, there is no existence other than his complete immersion in what he is living at the time—no past, no future. There is only the joy of the present.

Social scientist Mihaly Csikszentmihalyi has labeled this phenomenon "flow experiences," intrinsically rewarding moments in which there is "effortless action," in which the participant is so thoroughly involved in an activity that he or she performs at peak efficiency without conscious thought. But the minute you start thinking about what you're doing—while playing tennis, for example ("Watch my grip. . . . Keep my knees bent. . . . Aim for the backhand")—flow ceases. Peak experiences occur when you don't have to think about what you are doing; you just seem to do it better than you ever have before.

During the formulation of his theories on flow, Csikszentmihalyi interviewed a number of rock climbers similar to Jay. He believed that a solitary activity like climbing is perfectly suited for eliciting flow states: It requires complete concentration; if you think about anything else, you will fall. Furthermore, it is a task that involves one single person testing himself against an unyielding mountain. One rock climber he interviewed described his peak experiences:

> Climbing is unbelievably solo, [yet] the flow is a multitude of one. Climbing is dreamlike. When you're climbing, you're dealing with your subconscious as well as conscious mind. . . . You're climbing yourself as much as the rock. . . . If you're flowing with something, it's totally still. . . . There's no possibility of judging from the inside of a car whether the car is moving or the freeway. So you're not quite sure whether you are moving or the rock is, for the same reason, being inside yourself as you usually are. So it becomes very still. . . . Lack of self-awareness is totally self-aware to me. If the whole is self-awareness, you can have a lack of self-awareness because there's nothing else there.

Peak experiences during solitude often stimulate this flow state where you lose yourself in what you are doing. Certain other activities, especially outdoor ones that involve movement or communion with Nature (hiking, skiing, horseback riding), also lend themselves to complete immersion in the moment.

Whether you are alone in the woods, your car, or the bathroom, solitude provides opportunities for self-reflection. Just as you have a definite need to be with others, you have a desire to be with yourself, to have peak experiences without feeling lonely and alienated. A contented life is one that is filled with a balance of intimacy and solitude; without one, the other feels hollow. Solitude helps improve your productivity, inner wisdom, and independence; it allows you to face yourself without the need for distractions.

# 3

# Facing Yourself without Distractions

MARSHA VIBRATES WITH energy. She is bright, articulate, and speaks with such candor and intensity that she commands the full attention of others. She is competent, attractive, and successful. People naturally gravitate toward her because of her boundless enthusiasm and the love she so unselfishly shares with others.

Marsha finds it both surprising and frustrating that she has been without a serious relationship since her divorce a decade ago. She suspects it may have something to do with the desperation with which she has pursued her suitors; she senses their apprehensions but has been unable to moderate her ardor. Yet, even without a lover, she has managed to structure her life so that she is never by herself:

"When I'm alone I just end up feeling sorry for myself. I have so many regrets in my life. If only I hadn't tried so hard, I wouldn't have chased so many men away. If only I hadn't picked such a loser of a husband, perhaps my marriage wouldn't have been doomed to fail. If only I hadn't lost so many years drinking myself into a stupor to deny my mistakes. There are so many 'if onlys.'

"As you can tell, I don't like thinking about myself much, especially the past. When I'm alone, all this stuff comes back to haunt me. I realize how empty my life sometimes feels and how much I miss being involved with someone. But as long as I keep myself busy and spend time with friends, everything is just fine."

She considers herself an expert at avoiding being alone. By taking in a roommate, scheduling visitations with her child on specific days, and going back to graduate school, Marsha has insured she will not have a moment of solitude. Her principal strategy in life is to keep herself occupied in the social world and avoid her own company at all costs.

Given the importance of solitude to our overall well-being, why is it so hard for Marsha, and many others like her, to enjoy their own company without diversions? Why do we sometimes experience fear and apprehension during time alone? Why are other people sometimes threatened by our need to seek out solitude?

In this chapter we will explore many of the reasons why it can be difficult for us to spend time alone. While Marsha's attitude represents an extreme example of feeling uncomfortable during solitary periods of daily life, we have all been known to feel uneasy, lonely, bored, or anxious on occasion, and to find ways to ease the pain by diverting ourselves from our essential aloneness.

We will examine the avoidance of solitude within the context of the many biological, sociological, anthropological, and psychological forces that discourage solitary behavior. By becoming aware of the external and internal pressures that are working to undermine your enjoyment of time alone, you will be better equipped to counteract their stifling effects and to pursue more consciously the solitude that is so essential to your life satisfaction.

## THE HERDING INSTINCT

Nature provides tremendous insight into the biological basis for avoiding solitude. Quite simply, a sheep alone is a dead sheep. It is through the safety of the flock that foraging animals avoid annihilation. Until one member of a herd can be isolated from its brethren, a predator will not attack. A falcon, for example, unable to focus attention on a single target when there are other distractions crossing his field of vision, will conduct sham attacks merely to confuse and isolate a solitary prey from its companions.

Sociobiologists such as Georg Breuer believe that those animals who are the most successful staying in the middle of their packs, who have the strongest crowding instincts, have the best chances of survival. Since the offspring of these socially successful animals are those most likely to survive (those on the edge of the herd get picked off by predators before they have a chance to reproduce), evolution progressively strengthens the inborn tendency to remain in the company of others.

This herding instinct is so powerful in sheep that they will sacrifice the freshest grass on the fringes of the flock to stay huddled in a mass. Any solitary creature would soon be vulnerable to exhaustion without companions to share guard duty and hunting responsibilities. The same is true of the early settlers of any new region. Those who wandered too far from the stronghold, or who built their dwellings too far from the fort, were picked off by hostile enemies, while those who muscled their way into the center of their community were best protected.

We can also find examples of the herding instinct within our own culture. The value of real estate is usually related to its proximity to the center of commerce. The way we dress, the cars we drive, the things we aspire to own, are intended to make a statement of individuality, but always within the safe parameters of what is considered fashionable. Anyone who lives too far away from others is labeled a hermit. Anyone who departs too far from acceptable standards of conduct is considered odd or even potentially dangerous.

## SOCIAL CONDITIONING AGAINST SOLITUDE

In addition to biological instincts that create pressures for us to remain attached to the group, there are deeply ingrained cultural pressures that keep us connected to the larger fabric of society. Historians, anthropologists, and sociologists such as Joseph Bensman and Robert Lilienfeld have noted that ancient societies never distinguished between private and public worlds. The individual was so enmeshed in an extended family and tribal system that all behavior was monitored closely by others. It was inconceivable that anyone could have an identity separate from that of the community.

Indeed, the luxury of solitude would seem incomprehensible to those whose very survival requires interdependent vigilance. In preliterate societies, being alone has always been considered unnatural. A person alone is a danger because he or she feels temporary immunity from the constraints of government and is more likely to engage in behaviors that are not socially sanctioned.

Among the American Puritans, neighbors had the duty of "holy watching," a responsibility to observe and report any deviant or unusual behavior that might undermine the rigid social structure. Laws were passed forbidding anyone from living alone in order to suppress behavior that was "inconsistent with the mind of God." Even in the nineteenth century there was a general fear, expressed by voices as radical as Walt Whitman's, that solitary people would succumb to masturbation, the "master vice" thought to lead to everything from respiratory disorders to insanity.

Among the African Dobu tribe, anyone found alone is indicted for plotting against the well-being of others. It is believed there is no good reason for anyone to be alone except to plan some mischief that could undermine the delicate fabric of an interdependent society. Social scientists

Mihaly Csikszentmihalyi and Reed Larson explain how this avoidance of being alone evolved:

> In many cultures, being alone is feared, not because of physical dangers, but for more mysterious psychic threats that hatch and fester in solitude. The man who keeps to himself is suspected of sorcery. The woman who prefers to be alone is surely a witch. And the poor innocents who against their will find themselves alone, are naked prey to magical powers. It is not just being alone that is dangerous, but any attempt to separate oneself, in thought as well as in body, from one's kin. The notion of individuation, the effort to differentiate oneself from the group, which is so central to the Western idea of personal identity, has been viewed with distrust in most human cultures.

While we may be appalled at such oppressive control among so-called primitive peoples, we only have to look around our "developed" nations to find evidence of similar perceived threats to the stability of a society. Since governments can only be destabilized through secrecy and private plotting, in countries that are still developing their relatively young political systems, such as the Soviet Union and China, privacy is not tolerated much more than in the Dobu tribe.

Even within our own country, it is helpful to realize the extent to which the rules of society are enforced primarily through surveillance on individual privacy. What cameras, recording equipment, and busybodies can't pick up is compensated for by internal monitoring systems that are instilled at an early age. You can no doubt recall the shame you felt when you were caught picking your nose, biting your nails, or drawing on the wall. You can remember the tremendous pressure you felt in high school to be part of the group and the anguish you sometimes felt being an outsider. Even as an adult, people pressure you to conform to their desires: "What are you doing in there so long?" or "Wouldn't you rather join us?"

The discomfort you sometimes feel regarding your solitary activities is thus the result of deliberate programming by our culture. Emotions such as guilt, shame, and embarrassment are designed to keep you from deviating too far from sanctioned norms.

## THE SHADOW CAST BY SOLITUDE

It is apparent that private time has not been tolerated very well by human cultures that have been programmed over hundreds of generations to enforce compliance to group norms of togetherness. But the intense biological and social pressures are also reinforced by the profound existential issues activated when we are alone. In solitude we are forced to confront ourselves and all the pain, fear, doubt, and regret we carry deep within.

Each of us harbors within our mind a closetful of forbidden thoughts, scary feelings, repressed impulses, and uncomfortable memories. The door to this dark side is kept safely locked during most of daily life. It is when your defenses are down—after you've had a few drinks, when you are tired or dreaming, or when you are working in therapy—that you can smell and taste and feel any hidden wreckage. These thoughts and feelings come to haunt you when you are alone.

Consider, for example, the torture of a sleepless night. Every once in a while, for no reason you can easily discern, you find yourself tossing and turning, staring at the clock, waiting for sleep to come. Utterly alone in your struggle, your mind takes over. All your previous failures creep into consciousness. Your future looms bleakly. Your fears of the unknown, of rejection, of abandonment, of vulnerability, of dependence, of disease, all parade before your eyes.

Novelist Jim Harrison vividly describes the lonely and sometimes frightening experience of insomnia in which one cannot escape oneself:

> It was a night I would remember poignantly but not wish to repeat. Insomnia opens the door to previously untraced memories, makes a mockery of the good sense that possesses us at high noon, and any effort we make to channel our thoughts twists the energy, rebukes us with half-finished faces, sexless bodies; we learn again that our minds are full of snares, knots, goblins, the backward march of the dead, the bridges that end halfway and still hang in the air, those who failed to love us, those who irreparably harmed us, intentionally or not, even those we hurt badly and live on encapsulated in our regret. The past thrives on a sleepless night, reduces it to the awesome, distorted essence of all we have met.

Many people experience similar discomfort almost every time they find themselves alone for more than a few minutes without a planned activity. They are unable to entertain themselves, they lack the confidence and independence to take care of their own needs. Because they don't like themselves very much, they don't enjoy their own company. As a result, they will do almost anything to avoid the discomfort of being alone.

The theme of trying to escape solitude has been explored throughout literature, from Sophocles to Dostoyevsky, Joyce, Kafka, Camus, Conrad, and Salinger. Obsessed with themes of aloneness throughout his life, Thomas Wolfe describes the solitary condition of being human:

> Left alone to sleep within a shuttered room, with the thick sunlight printed in bars upon the floor, unfathomable loneliness and sadness crept through him: he saw his life down the solemn vista of a forest aisle, and he knew he would always be the sad one: caged in that little round of skull, im-

prisoned in that beating and most secret heart, his life must always walk down lonely passages. Lost. He understood that men were forever strangers to one another, that no one ever comes really to know any one, that imprisoned in the dark womb of our mother, we come to life without having seen her face, that we are given to her arms a stranger, and that, caught in that insoluble prison of being, we escape it never, no matter what arms may clasp us, what heart may warm us. Never, never, never, never.

On one level Wolfe is correct: We cannot possibly escape our essential aloneness. Trapped within our skin, encapsulated in a solitary identity, soul, mind, and body, we constantly search for strategies to escape our own "flesh-colored cage." In his book of that title, James Howard has observed: "Each of us exists within his own unique epidermal envelope as a separate thing. No other person can enter that envelope, nor can any of us escape from it. We were born in that enclosure, exist within it, and will wear it as our funeral shroud."

To bring this realization into awareness is to confront a profound aspect of human life. No wonder we often avoid being alone. For when we are physically alone we are face-to-face with the reality of our existential aloneness. We are forced to face the realization that deep down inside, there is no way we can ever fully connect with another being. This means that nobody else can ever understand you the way you know yourself; that relationships and intimacy with others only provide temporary relief from essential aloneness; and that to be alive is to experience occasional intense periods of loneliness and alienation from others.

To accept your existential isolation is to realize there is a separation between yourself and the world, "an unbridgeable gulf between oneself and any other being," according to psychiatrist Irvin Yalom. There is no way you can ever become fused with another; no matter what heights of intimacy you scale, you can never fully detach from your own solitary world. In this most basic of awarenesses you also are forced to confront another basic truth: You are ultimately responsible for yourself, and there is no way to absolve yourself of this awesome burden.

## ATTEMPTS TO ESCAPE ESSENTIAL ALONENESS

With our quest for material comfort and symbols of success, we distance ourselves from these understandings and distract ourselves from our essential aloneness. We devote so much time and energy to buying cars, houses, clothing, and jewelry that we don't get to know the private world within that is both wonderful and frightening.

I found it especially difficult to work with one client, a man driven toward the acquisition of things to escape aloneness. In fact, I didn't much care for this gentleman at all. I found my dislike disturbing, since it was getting in the way of my being more helpful to him. Yet, no matter how I would talk to myself, my stomach would start to churn as I listened to him brag about the Ferrari he had ordered, the new house he was building, the great meal he had eaten that was so incredibly expensive.

The sad thing was that his money and business successes brought him no peace; he was a singularly unhappy fellow who experienced only momentary contentment after buying his latest toy before he would slip deeper into a depression. He surrounded himself with others and could not stand even the thought of idle time alone. If there was no work in need of his attention, then there was shopping to be done.

During our sessions, I would attempt to escape from my feelings about him (and his issues) by retreating inside my own head. It was as if I couldn't stand to truly be with him, to listen to his story with compassion and understanding. I hated myself for my own contempt. And in the mental journeys I took to avoid this man who so desperately wanted my companionship, one of my favorite destinations was car shopping. I brought to mind visions of all the cars I would like to own, the merits of one over the other, how each would feel and sound and drive. I did this for weeks until one day, as the client was showing me his new solid-gold watch and I was out test-driving a Porsche in my head, I felt a cold chill on my neck. It finally occurred to me, as it must have to you, why I found it so difficult to be with this man: the things about him that I most despised were exactly those qualities in myself I feel most ashamed of.

This revelation became a turning point for both of us, especially after I shared my feelings with the client. He grew tremendously after getting honest feedback on how shallow his life was and how others must perceive him as I did—arrogant, self-centered, superficial. But I also got deeply in touch with my escape from self in the quest for an image to project—which, after all, is what cars are all about.

An equally common route of retreat from essential aloneness is to escape into books, films, radio, and, especially, television. These media not only provide entertainment but also act as distractions from yourself to help you avoid being alone and confronting unresolved personal issues. For example, the moment you enter your car, your first act after starting the ignition is to tune in the radio. Company at last. The radio blares news, sports, and music so you don't have to think about where you are going and why. If you're out on the road for a long run or bicycle ride, there is the trusty Walkman for company, filling your head with external stimulation to replace the emptiness you sometimes feel inside.

As long as there is another human voice around, even one echoing from an electronic box, you can avoid the fears associated with your aloneness. One researcher who studied this phenomenon discovered that the heaviest TV watchers were those who experienced the most anxiety when they were alone. Such people were plagued by disturbing thoughts and fantasies during private moments and so sought escape from their inner selves by diverting their attention onto some external source.

An attorney, who puts in fourteen-hour days at his office and still takes work home, shares his thoughts on this subject:

"I work hard. I deal with some very strange people in a very cutthroat business. It's a war out there. You either win or you lose; take no prisoners. When I'm not in court or working on files, I'm usually sitting in front of the TV. Mostly basketball and football games, but I'll watch any sporting event. If there's no sports on, I'll watch old movies. Hell, sometimes I'll watch anything! But I can't stand just sitting around staring at my belly button. When I get into a game, or a movie, or something, time just seems to fly by, and before I know it, it's time for bed and then another day begins."

It is not just the convenience of TV that leads the average household to keep it running seven hours per day: it's television's effectiveness in drowning out internal discomfort. Like this attorney, many people have a hard time dealing with unstructured solitary time; at the push of a button, laughter, excitement, and familiar faces fill the room. We are temporarily diverted from those feelings and memories we keep locked in our minds just out of consciousness.

Moreover, by identifying with characters on the screen or by escaping into an absorbing book, we become transplanted out of our skin into someone else's—usually someone more athletic, beautiful, talented, and loved than ourselves. We enter into "relationships" that are safe because they are strictly one-way and nonreciprocal; these "people" can never really hurt or reject us.

A young businesswoman told me that it is only when she is immersed in the pages of a book or involved in a television show that she feels freed of the weight of her thoughts:

"When I'm alone I brood a lot. I wonder where my career is headed, what people think of me at work. I fantasize what I would do if I had more money. I worry about what I would do if my husband died and how I would go on. I especially think about my kids and how I'm probably screwing them up. I wonder about all the ways I wish I could change my appearance—that my hair could be thicker or my thighs not so heavy. I just sit and think about these things unless I'm reading or something."

Of course, you cannot escape yourself indefinitely. Although some people try to distract themselves with work or television, or even alcohol or drugs, such strategies only work for a while. When you least expect it, you will feel your unresolved issues reposition themselves in your consciousness. Perhaps you will have trouble falling asleep or concentrating on your work. For no good reason that you can identify, you just feel funny—thoughts you've never considered before pop into your head uninvited. Things that used to give you pleasure suddenly feel empty. You begin yearning for something, though you don't know what it is. It no longer feels comfortable to be you, to be inside your body. If our bodies could talk to us they might very well make this speech:

"Look, dummy, you've been running away from yourself for a long time. You've been ignoring me, burying me, pretending I don't exist. You attempt to pacify me with diversions and distractions, anesthetize me, keep me quiet at all costs. It's so hard to get you by yourself so we can talk. Remember a few years ago when you were alone in the house with nothing to do? You couldn't get comfortable or find anything to occupy yourself. I tried to talk to you then. But first you switched on the TV for a while. Then you tried a book. You couldn't reach anyone by phone. You masturbated. That killed a half hour. But then I started whispering to you: 'Where are you going? Are you really happy with what you're doing? Take the time to know yourself.' You made yourself a stiff drink and that was that. But this time, kiddo, I'm not going away. I'm going to keep the heat up, keep the pressure on until you stop hiding from yourself, until you become truly comfortable in your own company. Sure you feel funny. You don't like what's happening in your body—the colds, the lethargy, the restlessness. But it's the only way I know to get your attention."

When we feel unusual symptoms it is usually for a good reason—even if it can't be identified. And one germ that lives deep inside each of us, resistant to all distractions, is the fear of being alone.

## PRIMAL FEARS OF BEING ALONE

Joseph Campbell, an expert on mythology, pointed out that the principal differentiating feature between animals and humans is our awareness of our own mortality and the steps we take to prepare for death. Throughout the ages, the creation of myth has provided comfort for this struggle.

The world's cultures and religions share a universal vision regarding death and afterlife that provides some degree of reassurance to those who are fearful of being alone in the unknown. From the Old and New Testaments to the hieroglyphics inscribed on pyramids, there is a promise that the individual will not be left to wander alone after death. The Christian image of Heaven is a place populated with a community of peers. The Hindus believe that the dead can return to the land of the living. The Egyptian and Tibetan Books of the Dead, the legends of the American Indians, Greek mythology—all attest to an afterlife that includes the fellowship of others.

Our greatest fears are thus appeased by mythology and religion: dying isn't so awful after all, and even if we don't like it, at least we won't be alone. Thus the death transition is marked by community ceremony—a funeral—to send the dead off in style. There is a pervasive feeling among the living that the deceased is still with us, as we will always be with him or her.

Even as a child, long before you understood the concept and reality of death, you experienced the terror of abandonment. From the perspective of the very young child, when an object is hidden from view it ceases to exist. The six-month-old baby will not search for a favorite toy that has been taken away—in the infant's mind, it is gone forever. You can then appreciate what it must have been like when your parents walked out of the room, leaving you a prisoner in the crib, your infant brain forced to come to grips with the idea that mother and father might never return. Who cannot remember their fears as a child when left alone? Every sound and imagined shadow took on a special significance. Comedian Bill Cosby tells of spreading JELL-O over the kitchen floor to trip the dreaded Chicken Heart he imagined was coming to devour him in his solitary defenselessness. The primal fear of being alone comes not only from the belief that monsters will come to tear us apart, but also from the monsters within us.

If the child dreads aloneness because of the fear of abandonment, what are the monsters that stalk the solitary adult? Here are a few common images:

- "What if someday I just lose control? What if I just flip out, jump off a balcony for no reason at all?"
- "What if my life is a sham? What if all the things I think are so damn important don't mean anything at all?"
- "What if I'm not really who or what I think I am? What if people are really laughing behind my back?"
- "What if they find out about that time I screwed up? What if they come to take away everything I've worked so hard to build?"

- "What if my friends or spouse desert me? What if they discover what I'm really like inside?"
- "What if something should happen to my child or parent? How could I ever survive that?"
- "What if I have cancer or AIDS or some other incurable disease? What if I'm going to die today?"

This last question seems to evoke the most primal fear. In fact, the avoidance of being alone stems from early associations with birth and death. Regardless of how we attempt to pacify this primal fear—with immersion in productive work, with belief in an afterlife, with illusions of immortality—deep within the recesses of every human brain lies the absolute terror of nothingness.

At any moment, an artery could burst in your brain, or the roof above you could fall in. The heart is simply a muscle that will one day wear out. And, compared to the few billion heartbeats of time that you are alive on Earth, you will be dead for a very long time. These terrifying realizations confronting the fragility of existence are more easily kept under control when we are in the company of others. When we are alone, according to Paul Tillich, "we meet ourselves, not as ourselves, but as the battleground for creation and destruction."

It is in private that the forbidden is entertained. When alone, you are free to contemplate revenge, imagining acts you would feel terrible shame about if anyone knew of them. Poet Hugh Prather, for one, confesses this urge to be hurtful, but in a way designed to free him of its self-destructive nature: "Within me is the potential to commit every evil act I see being committed by other men, and unless I *feel* this potential I can at any moment be controlled by these same urges."

Such ideas and fantasies remain harmless and inconsequential unless you empower them through obsessive thinking. One woman I know, who loves her husband very much and feels deeply committed to their marriage, nevertheless is plagued by outrageous, explicit sexual fantasies about one of her husband's friends. Fearful of even thinking about the possibility, much less ever acting on her impulses, she avoids being alone whenever possible. When she is alone, she tries to keep herself so busy that she can turn her brain off.

Many people feel apprehension about the directions their thinking takes when they are by themselves. One computer expert, for example, is kind, sensitive, and passive, but he is frightened of the rage he feels inside. He becomes particularly agitated when the computer is down and he is forced to consider a blank screen, which he then mentally fills with images of obnoxious clients he wants to strangle or of one of the firm's arrogant partners, whom he imagines begging to die after ruthless torture. Other men and women report thoughts of harming those they love, vanishing into another identity, running through the streets naked, raping and murdering, violating every one of the Ten Commandments, and committing all of the Seven Deadly Sins.

Among the most painful of all private musings are suicidal fantasies, which can be fleeting notions during idle time, or a deadly serious preoccupation. Short of those who genuinely see no way out of their misery, who have developed a specific plan of self-destruction, some degree of suicidal thinking is familiar to most people at pivotal times during their lives. And, as is evident in the case of one woman, even if there is relatively little danger of acting on the impulses, the images alone can be absolutely terrifying:

"It started out for me as a harmless mental exercise while driving on the freeway. What if I just jerked the steering wheel a notch—it wouldn't even have to be that much—and rammed into a tree? All my troubles would be over. I don't think I would ever do that, but sometimes it seems so easy. Then it's so hard to get rid of the image of crashing and burning, I avoid driving alone at night so I won't even be tempted."

We all have our individual tolerances for enjoying solitude while keeping our primal fears at bay. Some people literally can't stand more than an hour of being in their own company without feeling fearful or anxious; others can easily spend a month free of human contact without unpleasant effects. The degree to which we can tolerate, and even revel in, our solitude is directly related to our having confronted our fears and having become comfortable with our inner self. For anyone who wants to live fully and consciously, this confrontation is an essential step on the path of personal growth.

## DECLARATIONS OF INDEPENDENCE

In light of the strong external and internal pressures propelling us away from solitude, it is understandable why it is often so difficult to face ourselves without distraction. At the same time, it is easy to cave in to others' demands for our time and energy, to relinquish our independence and personal desires in favor of those imposed by our peer group. An example of this phenomenon is illustrated by a social worker who wished to get away from his professional and personal obligations for a while:

"I went to a popular singles resort in the Caribbean for a week of relaxation. The first morning there I needed some time to unwind a bit, so while others were scurrying off to yoga, water aerobics, sailing lessons, or volleyball games, I found a tree to sit under that had a great view of the bay.

"In the hour that I attempted to watch the water, I was approached by no less than three different staff members who asked me what the matter was, why I wasn't having fun, and wouldn't I rather join a group activity? It was inconceivable to them that I could be thoroughly happy simply being in my own company. I was so badgered to join in 'having a good time' that I eventually relinquished the solitude that others found so disturbing. The rest of the week I acted more 'appropriately' by participating in the various activities, all the while wishing I could get back home and at least enjoy the privacy of my car."

All of us often face strong pressures to give up our private moments and secret selves. Just think about all the obligations you feel—to your family unit as well as to your family history, your neighborhood, occupational affiliation, political party and civic organizations, social clubs, religious group and ethnic heritage, your county, state, and nation. This doesn't include all the informal friendship groups, bowling leagues, or bridge clubs. Everyone and every group seems to want a part of you.

To survive as a species, it is sometimes necessary for the individual to give up his or her freedom and independence for the greater good of the majority. This might involve donating time to charitable organizations, or working for a social service organization at a lower rate of pay than would be earned in the private sector.

Ironically, the result of these external pressures to contribute time, energy, and money is a genuine need to temporarily withdraw from such obligations. You start to feel closed in, resentful of all intrusions. You may desperately yearn to spend some time in your own company, doing whatever you wish. But if others perceive this sanctuary as lasting too long, the phone calls will start once again: "Gee, we haven't seen you for a while. What's the matter?"

Of course, the solitary activities we can most easily justify to ourselves are those that can be rationalized as unselfish. Among the Fulani of West Africa, a person will volunteer to lead cattle to the salt licks when he requires time alone. In our own culture, it is perfectly acceptable for someone to spend time alone knitting a sweater, tuning up an engine, cutting the grass, writing a novel, sometimes even fishing and hunting. Such activities are done supposedly to save money or to put food on the table. But any person caught sitting in the dark is often viewed with concern, suspicion, or resentment. The natural question will be asked: "What are you doing?" Or, even better, "Isn't there something you *should* be doing?"

You may occasionally declare your independence from group pressures, but it will usually be at some emotional cost. After all, eons of genetic programming have gone into ensuring your compliance with social responsibilities. You feel guilty if you don't contribute. Just as our early ancestors would have encountered repercussions if they decided to go for a walk instead of helping their tribe hunt game for the next meal, you are likely to experience some remorse, if not social disapproval, if you choose to do only what *you* want to do. Thus you may be caught between longings for time to yourself and the pressure to fulfill social obligations. This conflict is not only the result of biological herding instincts and societal pressures, but also of the age-old war between the rights of the individual versus those of the community. Throughout history there has been a struggle between the human need for freedom, independence, and autonomy versus the cultural values of cooperation, compromise, and sharing.

Social historian Barrington Moore points out this intrinsic conflict: "Without society there would be no need for privacy." Whereas society would not survive unless people are willing to give up a certain amount of privacy, it is difficult for any individual to survive without periods of solitary rejuvenation—even if only to continue efforts toward social productivity.

We are therefore pressured to avoid taking care of our own solitary needs, especially when the interests of society are in any way compromised. Consider the fate of Socrates, who declined to serve a political office in the public sector in favor of private meditation and reflection. Athens could not tolerate social criticism or eccentricity very well, so they served solitary dissenters lethal cocktails of ridicule and hemlock.

Our society has come a long way since the repressive regimes that were so intimidated by human rights and individual freedom. Most of North America was founded by people who yearned for the freedom to practice their religious convictions or to exercise their personal rights. Our ancestors were a fiercely independent lot who didn't take kindly to federal interference or the creation of laws that limited the individual's freedom to enjoy solitude. The American Declaration of Independence contains the dramatic statement: "We hold these Truths to be self-evident, that all Men are created equal, that they are endowed by their Creator with certain unalienable Rights, that among these are Life, Liberty, and the pursuit of Happiness." As if this wasn't enough, the Bill of Rights further protects privacy, individuality, and the right to say what we like, live where we want, and be protected from search, seizure, and violation of our personal territory and space.

For the first time in history, our society has been able to override its own fears and injunctions against solitude. We now know, based on many sources, that solitude is as essential a part of the structure of society as is participation. For the group, and for the individual, this is a paradox. Our ability to function best within the group and with others is contingent upon our abilities to navigate within ourselves.

Private moments are not a luxury but a requirement for optimal mental health. We require time alone to process new experiences, to think through our choices and make decisions, to relax and replenish energy, to experience our freedom in a world full of restrictions.

## A COMMITMENT TO DEVELOPING YOUR PRIVATE SELF

Although it is difficult to strive for greater independence and solitary satisfaction, it is a noble and necessary mission. You can expect a certain amount of internal and external resistance, and, armed with this knowledge, you can prepare yourself for the ongoing battles that lie ahead. You can then appreciate just how challenging is the task of becoming comfortable with a part of yourself that has been programmed over many generations to keep you fearful. After all, throughout the history of our planet, any creature separated from its tribe or herd did not survive for long.

Solitude represents a rare communion with your private self, an opportunity to confront and deal with your primal fears and secret self. It helps you move beyond ordinary consciousness into a deeper awareness of your existence and a clearer vision of the directions you are headed.

This proved to be true for Marsha, the woman whose words began this chapter. After several months in therapy, she became increasingly committed to pursuing a life free from dependencies on others and filled with more enjoyment of her private moments:

"I am tired of running from myself, of needing a man in my life to be happy. I am sick of feeling so damn uneasy every time I have free time I don't know what to do with. I have decided that finding a husband is not the answer for me. Instead I've got to learn to really enjoy being by myself. I want to go into a movie or restaurant alone and not care what others think. Already I can feel myself rebel against almost everything I was taught growing up: I will *not* live my life to make a man happy. And I *will* spend more time alone—and like it a lot!"

# *4*

# *Coping with Private Moments*

WHILE BEING ALONE can feel uncomfortable, it need not remain so. To reap the benefits of solitude and minimize the inhibiting effects of the primal fears of being alone, you must overcome your own inertia. This immobility is caused, in large measure, by the attitude you adopt. If you choose to feel helpless and trapped in your time alone, loneliness and boredom will surely result. On the other hand, if you are able to: (1) motivate yourself to think differently about your situation, (2) counteract negative feelings, (3) take risks of trying new behaviors, and (4) increase your tolerance for spending time in your own company, your private moments will become a sanctuary of tranquility and personal satisfaction.

## *INNER SPACE, INNER VOICES*

There is a place so private and inaccessible that you are the only one who will ever know it: that place is the private world inside your own mind. Although this inner space is completely isolated, there is constant companionship from your inner voice, which talks to you continuously—whispering, urging, blaming, reminding, encouraging, nagging, telling you what to do and how to feel about it. It forms the basis for many of your attitudes about the world and how you experience it. Unlike the intense existential issues and primal fears that are an intrinsic part of being human, many other difficult aspects of being alone, such as feeling bored or lonely, are shaped by these dialogues you have with yourself.

Every waking moment, some private conversation is going on inside you. You may be mindlessly repeating the words to a song or rehearsing a conversation. You may be calming yourself down or revving yourself up. Endlessly, you engage in conversation with yourself, safely expressing your dreams, fantasies, wishes, desires, and fears. This is privacy at its most secure and sacred—whether you are alone in the woods or squeezed into a crowd. Sometimes your inner voice can be incredibly cruel and judgmental:

- "I can't believe you said something so stupid."
- "That pimple has taken over your whole face."
- "You'll never get this right."
- "You really blew it, and everyone will find out."

Because we are with our private selves every moment, very little slips by us. Every imperfection is magnified a hundred times. We are obsessed with our flaws and mistakes because we know every one of them.

This inner space is a world forever hidden from others' view. In fact, some of us are so different on the inside from how we appear to others, the people who think they know us best would be surprised to discover the nature of our secret selves. It is not necessary, nor probably even desirable, that we compromise this inner space by disclosing more of it to others. Those who feel the need to confess can do so to a priest, therapist, spouse, or friend. It is not revelation we are after; rather, it is self-acceptance.

To attain a degree of congruence between the smooth, controlled character we show on the outside and the agitated character who lives inside, it is necessary to befriend our inner voice and make it more constructive. Unlike the awesome social pressure and core existential issues we must learn to live with, there are a number of negative feelings that are within our power to neutralize.

## THE DISTRESS OF BOREDOM

Described by the philosopher Kierkegaard as "the nothingness which pervades reality" and "the root of all evil," boredom inflicts more suffering on the human race than any other condition of being alive. Boredom drives the human spirit to distraction; it is restlessness in action, hollowness, emptiness, discontent, the anguish of energy without purpose.

Of all the stresses and strains of being alive, boredom is the most insidious. Voltaire spoke of it as "the worst of all conditions," a belief shared by other writers (such as Dostoyevsky, Ibsen, Nietzsche, Pascal, Beckett, Baudelaire, and Flaubert) who have been obsessed with the kind of torment described by one man:

"I have struggled my whole life with boredom, with feeling restless and frustrated, longing for some kind of action but not knowing how to create it. I feel bored by my work, which is just the same old crap over and over again. I feel bored with my marriage—we have so little to say to one another anymore. We only stay together because it is too much aggravation to separate. My friendships feel boring— we always do the same things, play golf or cards or drink. But most of all, I feel bored with myself. I can't stand being alone for more than an hour. I pace the floor. I watch TV. I try to read. I call people on the phone. When all else fails, I smoke a joint. Then at least things are a little more tolerable.

"I don't know how many shrinks I've seen to get to the bottom of my discontent. But I find therapy boring and self-indulgent. I talk about myself—the same old shit—and the therapist just pretends to be interested. I don't know how anybody could do that job listening to people whine all day. At least I can tell people to shut up and get out of my office."

Of all the difficulties in coping with private moments, boredom is the most common and therefore the most innocent. Who, after all, has not felt bored at some time during the past few days, or hours, or even minutes? Boredom becomes intolerable only when your inner voice betrays you, when you can find no outlet or diversion and have lost all incentive to find one. As seventeenth-century philosopher Blaise Pascal has written:

> We seek rest by struggling against certain obstacles and once they are overcome, rest proves intolerable because of the boredom it produces. . . . We think either of present or of threatened miseries, and even if we felt quite safe on every side, boredom on its own account would not fail to emerge from the depths of our hearts, where it is naturally rooted, and poison our whole mind.
>
> Man is so unhappy that he would be bored even if he had no cause for boredom, by the very nature of his temperament, and he is so vain that, though he had a thousand and one basic reasons for being bored, the slightest thing, like pushing a ball with billiard cue, will be enough to divert him.

However, boredom does have its benefits in promoting transitional periods of revitalization. It rests and relaxes us, allows time for momentum to recharge itself. In the words of psychologist Sam Keen, it is an opportunity "to strip away our character armor, shed layer after layer of imposed motivations and values, and circle closer to our unique essence."

A good example of how boredom can be harnessed for productive purposes is the case of Joshua Slocum, who in 1895 became the first man to circumnavigate the globe solo. At age fifty-one he set out in a thirty-seven-foot sloop and spent three years and 46,000 miles alone at sea. At one point, after spending seventy-two consecutive days without sight of man or beast, he remarked: "I was not distressed in any way during that time. There was no end of companionship; the very coral reefs kept me company, or gave me no time to feel lonely, which is the same thing."

During his solitary voyage Slocum encountered hostile natives, sharks, high winds, storms, pirates, defective equipment, jagged reefs, sickness, and shortages of supplies, yet ironically, nothing gave him as much difficulty as fair weather. When Slocum had little to do but rest and enjoy the ride, loneliness would creep in. After a while, the next crisis or adventure became a welcome relief. It was a struggle to fight the ocean tides, but it was worse to deal with whispered voices from the past. Slocum found boredom more pervasive than the threat of being capsized. Never did he imagine that he was setting out on a mission that would present more psychological obstacles than physical ones. But of all the exotic places he visited, Slocum's greatest accomplishment was the exploration of the uncharted seas within his own mind.

The pain of discontented aloneness sparks a search for greater self-understanding and self-intimacy. It is thus a period of self-scrutiny in which restlessness motivates action, dissatisfaction breeds change. This is true in coping with not only boredom and inertia, but even more uncomfortable feelings associated with being alone.

## THE EXPERIENCE OF LONELINESS

If boredom is the most common negative consequence of maintaining poor attitudes about being alone, then loneliness is the most painful. Like most other difficulties encountered in solitary experiences, loneliness results as much from self-destructive beliefs as it does from external circumstances. In her book on the subject, Louise Bernikow has observed that, similar to boredom, loneliness results from not knowing how to occupy one's time when alone.

One woman describes the excruciating anguish she has created for herself in not knowing what to do with herself:

"I feel this incredible pain, right about here in my heart. It's an aching feeling, an intense longing to be with somebody. And yet I feel so discouraged and helpless because I can't think of anyone to call or be with. It seems like all my relationships exist because of my persistent efforts. If I don't call someone, or initiate getting together, it feels like nobody in the world would ever reach out to me.

"This past weekend, for example, I wanted to go to the ballet so badly. And I even started to get dressed to go by myself. But then I thought of what it would feel like to walk into the auditorium alone, to see everyone else paired off chatting happily away. I thought about how uncomfortable I would feel during intermission with nobody to talk to. And then I realized I would be making a long drive home alone, with nobody to share the experience. I took off my clothes, put on my bathrobe, got into bed with the covers pulled over my head, and cried myself to sleep."

These words, spoken by a woman who has yet to adjust to divorce after seven years of struggle, poignantly illustrate the pain of intense loneliness. Researchers such as James Lynch and Ronald Glaser have even found that loneliness can be lethal! Those who are isolated, or feel alienated and lonely, can literally die of a broken heart. The recently widowed have ten times the risk of heart failure compared to those who retain their companions. People who are single or divorced similarly experience greater physical risks; the immunological systems of lonely people have a greater tendency to break down, making them more susceptible to disease.

Many people associate the experience of loneliness with the elderly. However, it is not just the aged who are vulnerable. In fact, feelings of loneliness progressively *decline* with age. A college student, for example, is four times more likely to feel lonely than a senior citizen, even though the elderly are more likely to live alone and have fewer friends. Researchers at New York University believe this discrepancy results from the young person's unrealistic, idealistic, and romantic expectations for a partner or friend. The young are more frustrated than the old in their search for intimacy because they expect and demand more from others.

It is evident that while many people use the word "lonely" to describe how they feel, there are at least a half dozen different conditions to which the word could be applied. Physician and human ecologist J. Ralph Audy distinguishes between episodes of loneliness that are a normal part of existence, and states of loneliness that are more intense and chronic. He further describes pathological loneliness as voluntary social withdrawal of an extreme nature, usually accompanied by self-pity, listlessness, depression, and inconsolable grief. The last of these symptoms is described from one woman's unusual point of view, emphasizing her acceptance of things as they are:

"One of the things I do when alone is to allow myself to experience grief openly and as fully as it emerges. My grief feelings encompass levels of felt loss—from the death of a loved one to seeing my life/time being used up, to people moving away, to the realization that possibilities will never become real and illusions, once gone, are gone forever.

"The grief emerges with such a crashing wavelike force, such a searing feeling of pain in the middle of my chest, that I am astounded by its intensity and suddenness—it is such a physical contracting, constricting, twisting of my insides and I wonder what muscles are there—these muscles that tense and churn and find release in sobs or sighs or anger. Sometimes it is felt more in my throat, this tightening and closing off—I think I try to close off from feeling it, but it usually doesn't work so I allow it and own it and that somehow makes it go away.

"The grief and loneliness happen in response to a memory—triggered by outside events or internal wanderings. Sometimes I engage in these inner journeys because I feel a need to go further into the feelings, work through them to a different level, a different quality. Letting myself experience this despair is among the most painful things I have ever lived through, yet it is from this anguish that I have learned the most."

This woman testifies to the potential of loneliness for producing growth as well as devastation. The particular direction loneliness takes seems to depend on its principal underlying cause. When researchers Carin Rubinstein and Phillip Shaver surveyed 25,000 people as to the reasons they felt lonely, several factors were cited.

*Inactivity.* As with boredom, the greatest difficulty people report about loneliness is that of inactivity, restlessness, and undirected energy. Once you are occupied again, distracted, moving in a particular direction, loneliness dissipates into the background, waiting for the next idle period.

*The empty house.* The second most common situation that people report as instigating loneliness is coming home to an empty house. As long as you are out in the world, acting and reacting, buying and selling, conducting the business of daily life, you have at least the illusion of interconnectedness to others. All day long you deal with people, on the phone or in person. A neighbor waves a greeting as you leave for work. A dog barks at you, wags its tail. You buy a paper and the cashier smiles and says, "Have a good day." Interaction with co-workers or customers, acquaintances or friends, all sorts of human contact during the day, lead you to believe you are an integral part of the functioning world. People care. You are important, needed, bonded to others.

Then you walk through the door of your empty home into utter stillness. Nobody to greet you, welcome you into open arms. No smells of dinner cooking. No movement or human life. Just plants and bills waiting. It is then, for many people, that feelings of loneliness start to creep through.

*Marital status.* The third most prevalent reason for feeling lonely is marital status. With all the complaints and criticisms that people utter about feeling trapped in marriage, it does provide considerable insulation from loneliness. Single people, especially those who are not currently involved with someone, are a lot more likely to feel lonely than their married friends. They miss domestic routines that are so much a part of a comfortable relationship. They often long for greater physical contact—not only sexual intimacy, but also simple physical affection—hugs, warm touches, back rubs. They miss the ongoing security of a relationship and a commitment for the future.

*Feeling misunderstood.* A fourth stimulator of loneliness is the feeling of being misunderstood by others. Imagine, for example, you are at a social gathering where you feel awkward because you know very few people. You attempt to make eye contact with a few people who seem interesting. They avert their gaze, believing you are flirting. You try to join a conversation in progress but are at first ignored. You bide your time, waiting for an opening to express an opinion. Then it becomes apparent you have misinterpreted the topic under discussion. You sheepishly melt back into the crowd.

Feeling misunderstood by strangers is not half as bad as when it occurs within your most intimate circle. Nevertheless, loneliness inevitably results from the temporary or permanent realization that you are different from others, that your values and views are not readily embraced by the outside world. You stand alone in your beliefs, and that feeling sometimes becomes quite lonely.

*Shyness.* People most likely to feel lonely tend to be shy, quiet, withdrawn, introspective; they make themselves invisible. To make matters worse, they have a style of inner dialogue that keeps them isolated, discouraged, and demoralized.

*Intense feelings.* Lonely people especially feel states of anger, boredom, depression, frustration, and impatience. All of their negative emotions seem magnified.

*Irrational thinking.* Lonely people exhibit a cognitive style steeped in self-critical judgments. They misinterpret social cues, misjudge the meaning of others' behavior, and are prone to exaggerations and distortions of reality. They devalue their own accomplishments, yet are cynical and mistrustful of others.

*Ineffectiveness.* The lonely may appear withdrawn and inaccessible. They have deficits in social skills and are unable to create opportunities for interacting with others. They are unduly self-focused and unresponsive. Generally, they have a difficult time dealing with other people; and they often perceive in a dismal light those experiences they do have with others.

## REFRAMING LONELINESS AS ACTIVE SOLITUDE

One of the most effective ways in which people can cope with feelings of loneliness is by reframing their loneliness as an active form of solitude. The underlying grief or pain is then seen as having some meaning; it may even be a necessary form of suffering that acts as a transition for further growth. Further, it is important to give yourself hope, realistic expectations that things can and will be better.

In his work on cognitive treatments of depression, Jeffrey Young has identified several examples of internal self-statements that specifically exacerbate loneliness, but which can be modified instead to help minimize it:

- "I'll always be alone."
- "I can't change the way I am."
- "I can't stand being alone."
- "Life has no meaning without someone to share it with."
- "Nobody understands me."
- "Men/Women can't be trusted."
- "It's not worth the trouble meeting others; they'll just disappoint you."
- "I'm better off being alone than risking being hurt again."
- "Other people don't like me."

Even the diagnosis "I'm lonely" is a judgment about how you are feeling. The same situation—walking into an empty house, being alone at a party, having unstructured time— can be interpreted in a number of different ways depending on your outlook. Those who are prone to loneliness are quick to label themselves in terms of discontent. Those who are relatively immune to lonely feelings are those who have purged the word, if not the concept, from their vocabu- laries. They no longer even treat "loneliness" as a distinct feeling; rather they have reframed it as a variation of per- ceived dissatisfaction.

Another factor that is useful in coping with loneliness is to give personal meaning and purpose to your pain. Those who are widowed, divorced, or abandoned feel differently about their time spent alone than do monks, explorers, and writers who have deliberately *chosen* solitude. Even people whose circumstances are similar can feel quite differently about the experience. Contrast, for example, the plight of one recently divorced man who is embittered, helpless, de- spondent, and completely at a loss as to what to do, and a woman who has also lost her spouse against her will but feels there is some value in learning to adapt, to live inde- pendently, to prove she can take care of herself.

Even when loneliness can't be avoided, it can still stimulate growth. Because of its intrinsically uncomfortable qualities, loneliness acts as a warning system that something is out of balance. Similar to a fever or any physical symptom that signals disequilibrium in the body, loneliness motivates the human organism to restore balance in solitary/social functioning. It can be a kind of constructive pain that, once understood and interpreted accurately, enables you to act more decisively, to take interpersonal risks, and to initiate social contact. Although loneliness may be an unavoidable condition of being human, it can be, in the words of psychologist Clark Moustakas, a necessary step before personal transformation can take place:

> There is power in loneliness, purity, self-immersion, and depth which is unlike any other experience. Being lonely is such a total, direct, vivid existence, so deeply felt, so startlingly different, that there is no room for any other perception, feeling, or awareness. Loneliness is an organic experience which points to nothing else, is for no other purpose and results in nothing but the realization of itself. Loneliness is not homelessness. There is no departure or exile, the person is fully there, as fully as he can ever be.

## CHANGING THE WAY YOU TALK TO YOURSELF

It should now be clear that negative solitary experiences such as boredom and loneliness are primarily the result of how you choose to think about your situation. To change your attitudes and thereby feel more positive about your aloneness, you can learn to talk to yourself differently about what you are experiencing. Compare, for example, the ways two people might respond internally to several situations.

Phillip and Marcie, although they have never met, are in similar predicaments. Each lives alone and is not currently involved in a romantic relationship. However, we can see that they differ in their patterns of self-talk in response to various common occurrences.

## A Sunday Night with Nothing to Do

### Phillip

"There's nothing to do and nowhere to go. I just can't stand this much longer."

### Marcie

"Finally some time to relax. How great it feels to have some unscheduled time to do absolutely nothing."

## A Reminder of a Previous Love Relationship

### Phillip

"How could she do this to me? I'll never find anyone else to love me again. It's just not worth trusting other people; they only betray me in the end. I hate being alone, but I won't ever risk loving anyone that much again."

### Marcie

"I feel sad that things didn't work out the way I wanted. But I know if I'm patient, if I take care of myself, if I get on with my life, eventually I will meet someone else just as precious."

## Being Alone in a Social Situation

### Phillip

"This is awful. I never know what to do in these situations. These people look like jerks anyway. If I approach someone she'll just laugh at me. God, I hate this. Why did I ever come?"

### Marcie

"This is tough. Time to take a deep breath and jump in. There's somebody who looks interesting. What's the worst he can say to me? Whatever he does, it can't be any worse than standing here feeling helpless and awkward. Well, here goes. . . ."

## A Restless Night

### Phillip

"This is so frustrating tossing and turning. I'll never get to sleep and then I'll be a wreck tomorrow. Being alone is worse at night. I just keep thinking about how things went wrong, again and again. I should have. . . ."

### Marcie

"Can't seem to get to sleep. I wonder what's bothering me? Well, there is no use worrying about something I can't control. There is no sense in torturing myself lying awake in bed. Maybe I'll soak in a hot bath for a while and then read a bit."

## Engaging in a Harmless Solitary Habit

### Phillip

"If anyone ever knew I did this they'd think I was nuts. I feel so guilty afterwards, but I can't seem to stop. Why am I so weak? And why can't I just let myself enjoy a few simple pleasures?"

### Marcie

"It feels so good to just be myself when nobody else is around. I feel completely free to be or do whatever I like whenever I want. This is fun!"

Given their inner dialogues, there is no doubt that these two individuals would react quite differently to identical situations. Whereas Phillip feels lonely, depressed, and helpless because he thinks so negatively about the situations he faces, Marcie chooses to interpret these same events in a radically different way.

Cognitive theorists such as Albert Ellis, Aaron Beck, David Burns, and Jeffrey Young have worked extensively teaching people to think more rationally, calmly, and productively about the life events they encounter. Based on extensive research over the past forty years, these psychologists and psychiatrists have identified several principles of rational thinking. We saw examples of them in Marcie's internal dialogue. To develop a strategy of rational thinking, you must follow several sequential steps that involve asking yourself a series of questions:

**1. *How do I feel about this situation, and is that feeling OK with me?***

"I'm feeling anxious and restless and frustrated and angry, and no, that's not OK. I don't wish to feel this way. And it's my choice to interpret what is going on in a manner that allows me to be in more control."

**2. *What irrational things am I saying to myself?***

"Why is this always happening to me?"

"Life just isn't fair."

"This is terrible and I'll never make it."

"I need to be involved with someone in order to be happy."

"There's nothing to do."

"I'm so alone."

**3. *What can I say to myself instead that seems more appropriate and consistent with reality?***

"Things like this don't *always* happen to me; it just appears that way because I'm upset. In fact, this is a relatively rare event in my life that I'm simply exaggerating."

"That's right—life isn't fair. If it were, I would always get what I want whenever I choose. But it isn't bad luck or fate that put me in this mess—I did it myself, so only I can pull myself out of it."

"This is hardly as awful as I am making it out to be. Sure, it is uncomfortable and unfortunate that I can't have what I want, but it is hardly the tragedy I am making this out to be."

"I don't actually *need* to have a lover to be happy; it would just be a nice addition to my life. Actually, I can and will manage quite nicely as a single person."

"It just feels like there is nothing to do right now; however, it is my laziness and inertia that is allowing me to sit on my butt and wait for something to happen. If I have nothing to entertain myself with at this moment, it is because I haven't yet invested the energy to create something fun or productive."

"In one sense I am alone, but not to the extent that I am telling myself. Just because nobody called doesn't mean I don't have friends and family who care deeply about me. And if I don't have the quality of relationships that I would like, it is my own fault for not initiating greater depth and closer communication."

"Big deal that things didn't work out the way I anticipated. I can still make the best of the situation by accepting things the way they are instead of demanding them to be different."

"I'm letting myself get upset about something that is relatively insignificant in my life. Who will know about this, or care, a hundred years from now?"

The implications of the internal strategy demonstrated here are profound: You can counteract the negative feelings you have about being alone by changing the way you think about your life circumstances. With disciplined study and practice, it is possible to interpret the world in a more positive light and to view your own life situation in a way that permits greater internal control. A prime tool is to change the manner in which you talk to yourself. Self-statements, such as those previously described, can help you to feel better about yourself, thus helping you to be more willing to try risking alternative ways of acting and being.

## RISK-TAKING

J. and V. Rosenbaum, authors of a book entitled *Conquering Loneliness,* concluded that those who are dissatisfied during their time alone are more passive than they need to be. They are reluctant to take an active role in making things happen in their lives, and they especially avoid taking risks of any kind. This does not mean "risky" behavior in the sense of actions that jeopardize physical safety; it means those private experiences that are challenging on an emotional level because they require a degree of initiative or exploring the unknown.

Lonely people do not experiment with new behaviors, do not initiate new relationships, do not risk revealing themselves openly. They refuse to take responsibility for their plight and for the possibility that they can do something about changing it.

People avoid risks primarily because of fear of the consequences. Before attempting any new behavior, we are often crippled by doubts due to anticipating disaster. It is indeed the fear of failure that most inhibits our willingness to risk being different than we have been, to break out of the shell of isolation. It takes courage and determination to overcome fears of rejection, failure, and vulnerability, intimacy, to confront the inner storm inside us.

A case in point is the experience of one busy executive who has every waking hour of his life accounted for in various meetings, consultations, and social obligations. It recently occurred to him that even the simplest of solitary events, that of eating a meal alone in a restaurant, was beyond his immediate experience. With the impending prospect of an evening that was completely unscheduled— his wife was out of town—he decided it would be a useful exercise for him to go out to dinner alone. This may not seem like a very big risk, but to him it felt like uncharted territory, something he always wanted to try but had never taken the time to face.

"First, for people like myself who have very little experience being alone with nothing to do, it is definitely an altered state of consciousness. If I may make a comparison that seemingly makes no sense, it was like being in an isolation tank in public. The awareness of my own mental chat-

ter was tremendous. There was, as well, an ongoing flow of
emotional tide as my feelings about what was going on were
very much more engaged than what is usual for me—my
emotional reaction to the speed with which the waiter came,
my feelings of isolation when there was laughter at the table
next to mine, my hopes as I watched the door that someone
I knew would come in to the restaurant.

"Additionally, I was very much aware of levels of visual
perception as I began to look around in a way that I would
not when I was with someone else. All of this, I guess,
presents a picture of the value of time alone as a potential
teacher: it is an opportunity to come into contact with
oneself in the way that a writer might experience the activities of everyday life from a new perspective.

"I sense that this experience is very much like coming in
from the outside on a cold day and taking off first one layer
of outer garment, and then another, as one warms to the
room. I'm sure that as I choose to be alone more frequently,
the experience will change and other levels will be re-
vealed—perhaps as different from one another as a heavy
outer coat is from a T-shirt."

The metaphor of stripping off layers of garments as you
get closer to an inner core is indeed a fitting way to describe
the process of spending introspective time in your own
company. As time goes on, and slowly you feel comfortable
enough to remove another layer of protection, you become
more aware of what is going on around you and inside you.
And with each stage in this exploration, you become more
vulnerable.

There is a relationship between the risks you take, the
energy you expend in the pursuit of solitude, and the potential joy you can experience. The most difficult challenge of
all is to break loose from the bounds of your habitual patterns and predictable routines, to give yourself options you
have never considered before.

In the interviews I conducted with people about how
they spend their private moments, one of the areas I focused

on was those solitary activities that initially felt risky for them to pursue. In listing some of the favorite ways that people enjoy spending their solitude. I hope to stimulate your own motivation for pushing yourself to risk trying new activities and stretching the limits of what you consider comfortable. As you read through this list, some of the activities may not seem risky or difficult to you because they are already part of your repertoire. Others, however, may act as an impetus for you to expand your own solitary horizons.

## A Partial List of Solitary Activities That Feel Risky

*The Activity:* Studying a subject that has been difficult for you to understand (for example, calculus, organic chemistry, or phenomenological philosophy).
*The Risk:* That you will discover you can't understand it no matter how hard you try.

*The Activity:* Teaching yourself to overcome an area of ineptitude (for example, auto mechanics, gourmet cooking, or computer literacy).
*The Risk:* That you will confront the limits of what you can learn or manage.

*The Activity:* Signing up for court time at the racquet club just to practice your serve.
*The Risk:* That people will think you couldn't find anyone to play with.

*The Activity:* Writing down some of your worst fears and exploring their origins.
*The Risk:* That you will open up a lot of unresolved issues you don't really want to deal with.

*The Activity:* Going out to dinner at a fancy restaurant by yourself (variations of this include a concert, an opera, a play, a wedding).

*The Risk:* That someone you know will see you and feel sorry for you because you are by yourself.

*The Activity:* Taking up bicycling even though you've never been athletic before (variations include running, weight lifting, yoga, golf, cross-country skiing).
*The Risk:* That you will discover you don't have the coordination, stamina, or willpower to stick with it.

*The Activity:* Going to the park on a Sunday with nothing to do, just to fly a kite.
*The Risk:* That you will find it boring and silly and wish you had stayed home.

*The Activity:* Turning down a date on a Saturday night to stay home and catch your breath.
*The Risk:* That you won't get any other invitations for a long time.

*The Activity:* Taking a vacation by yourself.
*The Risk:* That you will have a lousy time, not be able to entertain yourself, or wish you had someone to share the experience with.

*The Activity:* Forcing yourself to stay home and do nothing at all—no TV, no books, no phone calls, no work—just sitting on the porch and relaxing.
*The Risk:* That you will be bored to death being in your own company without something to do.

Ironically, it is this last activity on the list, reported by several different people, that seemed the riskiest of all. The possible consequences of the other activities seemed manageable—that is, even if you did have a lousy time, if you weren't good at something you tried, if others did wonder why you were by yourself—those don't seem quite so devastating as having to confront the fact that, basically, you don't much like being in your own company. But even that circumstance can be overcome if you are willing to take the risk of learning to spend time with yourself and overcome feelings of anxiety, loneliness, or boredom. For some people, the only way they are going to learn to enjoy their own company is by experiencing some form of therapeutic isolation in which they are forced to encounter themselves.

## THERAPEUTIC ISOLATION

There are systematic ways in which to shed layers of protective armor in order to feel more comfortable with your unadorned, naked self. In a graduated series of activities geared to this, the simplest version is going for a walk by yourself. During such solitary interludes you are afforded the opportunity to clear your mind and metabolize the pressures of the day. More prolonged periods of isolation are possible within the context of overnight camping trips, retreats, or submersion in specially designed isolation tanks. There is even a form of psychotherapy based primarily on structured periods of isolation to increase the person's willingness to risk getting to know himself.

For example, a Japanese physician invented a form of therapy that promotes a oneness with Nature and society by counteracting feelings of isolation and alienation. This is accomplished, paradoxically, by blocking introspective thought, which often leads to self-criticism, by forcing the person to get outside of himself when alone. In Morita therapy, the client is separated from his egocentrism and narcissism, his obsessive focus on self to the exclusion of the natural world. The tenets of this treatment are useful because they help to counterbalance the excesses of introspection. Following the principles of Zen philosophy, negative feelings associated with being alone are dissipated by focusing energy and concentration outside the self. This provides an alternative for those who have discovered that, when in their own company, reflecting on the meaning of their personal existence creates only greater suffering.

Initially, the client is prescribed complete bed rest for a week—no visitors, books, radio, or television, nothing to write with. The person is left completely alone with his neurosis until he has accepted it as part of himself. Gradually, the client is moved from the immobility and seclusion of bed to the serenity of a garden, where he is permitted to work, then write in a journal about what he is experiencing. Eventually the Morita therapist becomes involved with the client in the garden, but not in the usual manner of sharing confidences, which would only once again emphasize self-centeredness, the essence of neurosis. Rather, attention is directed away from self to the world of Nature and of others.

As extreme as this treatment may appear, several principles of Morita therapy may be beneficial in everyday life:

- Spend one hour of time alone without distraction or diversions. Gradually expand the sessions to eight hours at a time.
- Monitor the amount of time you spend inside your head narcissistically obsessed with yourself. Direct your attention away from yourself to the world of other people and Nature.
- Practice writing each evening after a period of quietude. Note what you saw and what you did that day—especially the simplest things. Try to describe the way a cloud moves or the sound of a child's laughter.

Whether you employ a strategy that emphasizes greater detachment from your obsession with self, or one that helps you get closer to your inner core, theologian Paul Tillich offers some advice for coping with the negative feelings associated with being alone: "Loneliness can be conquered only by those who can bear solitude. We have a natural desire for solitude because we are men; we want to feel what we are, namely, alone, not as a matter of pain and horror, but as a matter of joy and courage."

The joy and courage that are so much a part of solitude flow naturally after you have successfully neutralized the fears, the boredom, and the loneliness discussed in the last two chapters. Changing the way you talk to yourself, taking risks, and increasing your threshold for time alone are certainly crucial steps in this endeavor. The chapters that follow are designed to help you continue this effort by focusing on specific qualities associated with satisfying and productive private moments.

CHAPTER

*5*

# *Being Self-Nurturing*

*T*HE VAST MAJORITY of private moments are spent engaging in the most ordinary of activities, things you do with neither fanfare nor much conscious attention. These include the routine chores of grooming yourself, taking care of various body functions, releasing stress and tension, and engaging in pleasurable acts. They are crucial to your ability to function effectively in the world. They are instrumental not only in making the outside of your body presentable to others, but also in soothing and nurturing the inside. Acts of self-nurturing thus represent that part of your private time in which you are solely concerned with taking care of your own desires and needs.

Although the self-nurturing behaviors explored in this chapter are practiced by virtually every member of the human race, they almost always take place in solitude. In the hundreds of conversations, interviews, and discussions I conducted in researching this book, time and time again it became evident that never before had these people shared aloud the ways in which they take care of their needs in their private moments.

People were surprised to discover that others, too, have intricate personal rituals involving bathing and grooming; have given careful consideration in their bathroom reading; having developed favorite food concoctions best eaten in private; or have perfected the art of going to the bathroom in the middle of the night without fully waking up! While these are ordinary private moments, they represent opportunities in which we are able to enrich our lives by taking better care of ourselves.

In this chapter you will learn about some of the common as well as eccentric ways that people enjoy their self-nurturing time alone. Such a survey will help you to realize just how important these solitary activities are in keeping you relaxed, groomed, entertained, and personally fulfilled. And you may be relieved, as well as amused, to learn that other people's secret selves and private moments are not so different from your own.

## THE FACE IN THE MIRROR

Approximately 10 percent of the time spent alone—up to several hours each day for some people—is occupied by personal grooming. Considering the billions of dollars spent annually on cosmetics, soaps, hair products, skin lotions, perfumes, and other hygiene products, it can be said that grooming is one of the most visible ways in which people nurture themselves. Much more than an effort to maintain health, these solitary activities represent attempts to look as youthful and attractive as possible.

Zoologist Desmond Morris has traced the evolution of grooming habits from a public form of greeting (primates say hello by picking at each other's fur), to an effort to maintain personal hygiene, to a private luxury of people making themselves appear more desirable to others. A clean-shaven face or a well-trimmed beard, an elaborately made-up face, a ring through the nose, a tattoo on the forehead—all were originally viewed as badges of prestige and status. For example, during ancient times, those women whose faces displayed complex arrangements of shadowing, highlighting, and color obviously had much leisure time to devote to the task of applying cosmetics.

During ancient times makeup was originally designed to offer protection against the sun. The Egyptians used eye makeup to reduce the glare of intense sunlight. Today, of

course, cosmetics are intended to make people look health-
ier, younger, and more attractive to the opposite sex. The
use of blush and lipstick, for example, unconsciously at-
tracts male attention by simulating the heightened coloring
of sexual arousal.

Many grooming tasks can be intrinsicially relaxing and
pleasurable. For one mother of three young children, the act
of polishing her nails during a few spare minutes provides
her with a feeling of self-nurturance:

"I like to do my nails when things are quiet around the
house, when everybody in my family is taken care of and
won't ask me to do something for them. Otherwise, I get all
relaxed and settled in and then I hear voices screaming up
the stairway: 'Mom, could you make me something to eat?'
'Mom, would you help me find my baseball cards?' 'Mom,
the dryer is buzzing!' 'Anita, could you help me move this
table?' 'Honey, could you read this letter and tell me what
you think?' God, it's enough to drive me crazy! You'd think
the world would end if I wasn't around to find misplaced
objects or make snacks.

"Anyway, when I polish my nails I try to isolate myself
from these demands. It gives me a lot of pleasure to spend
time alone doing something just for me. I like to look at the
finished product, the smooth polish. I can think about something else if I want to, or just concentrate on the activity
itself and watch the process, carefully taking the brush out
of the bottle, making sure there is just the right amount of
polish on the brush. Then wait for the nail to dry, carefully
testing it with my lips. Applying the second coat, wait, and
then finally the top coat. It feels wonderful when I'm
done!"

A salesman describes how he grooms himself as a form of
relaxation and pleasure after spending most of his day serv-
ing others. After calling on prospective customers, many of
whom have little interest in the products he is promoting,
he can't wait to get back to his apartment where, within the

privacy of his bathroom, he can replenish his energy and cleanse his aching soul.

"I get tired of dealing with other people, so sometimes I stay home and just nurture myself. I have these elaborate pampering sessions that last well into the night. First, I bring a radio into the bathroom and light several candles. Then I take a long, hot bath, soaking every ounce of tension out of my body. Sometimes, I even give myself a facial. By cleansing myself so thoroughly it feels like I'm making up for all the rejection I suffer during the week."

While these two people describe the use of private time in the intrinsic pleasures of the grooming process, much of the energy expended in grooming is done solely for its desired effect on others. Most people are self-conscious about the way they look, and no matter how good they might appear to others, they have a long list of things they wish they could change about their appearance. Thus, the mirror becomes a focal point for private life. Alone, it is permissible to examine your reflection without fear of being criticized for being too self-involved.

The day begins and ends for most of us in the privacy of the bathroom, studying the mirror for clues as to what, if anything, has changed about our appearance during the day or night. Alone, beyond the gaze of others, each square inch of our physical selves is explored, critically and unselfconsciously. The body is weighed, prodded, and examined. Inventory is taken of wrinkles, complexion, gray hairs, receding hairline, all without embarrassment.

Many people spend time in front of the mirror, looking critically at the person who stares back, and working diligently to make themselves appear in the best possible light. One woman spends time every day before the mirror, experimenting with different ways to change her appearance:

"I take out my comb and play with my hair, brush it out, change the part, experiment with different styles. I always check my eyebrows when I'm alone to see if any stray hairs have emerged. As I'm short in stature I am very conscious of people being able to see my eyebrows. I try to keep them groomed perfectly at all times. I also like to experiment with makeup. Each week I might buy a new lipstick or eye shadow or eyeliner. I will wait until I have a few minutes to try on the new product and see how it looks, how it combines with the makeup products I already have. First, I decide what kind of 'look' I want to create—something light and carefree, or something dark and sultry; depending on what color clothes I will be wearing and whether or not to match the eye shadow and eyeliner and mascara to it. Then I take out the products and do my face.

"The best part comes as I approach my closet. As I turn on the light and walk through, I scan the outfits lined up in their neat rows. Each one triggers a memory of where I bought it and for which occasion. I take out all the clothes I might wear in anticipation for a particular party and spread them out on the bed. I try them on one at a time, selecting jewelry and accessories, and look at myself in the mirror. Then, imagining my hair is perfectly done, I model different gestures I might use—a shrug of the shoulders, a full smile, a profile. Then I'll stand on my tiptoes to see the effect of wearing high-heeled shoes and go through my repertoire of movements again. I think about what other people will be wearing and whether this ensemble achieves the 'look' I am hoping for. Then I consider what my husband's reaction would be, what he would advise or recommend. And I smile to myself as I know one comment he will always make: 'That would look better without underwear!'"

For those who are reasonably satisfied with their appearance, like the woman above, sessions in front of the mirror are routine experiences. Yet for those who are self-conscious about their shape or features, solitary self-examination can be tremendously frustrating and depressing. Instead of focusing on maximizing their potential, such people turn their grooming sessions into intensely critical self-scrutiny in which they judge themselves against some ideal, some elusive standard of beauty. This is precisely the case with the woman below:

"I study my nose. Mostly, I'm used to looking at it in the mirror from the front, so when I look at it in a three-way mirror from the side, I'm horrified at how large it looks! I always think, at first, that it really cannot be this big. Then I look at it from the other side. I'm shocked again, but a little less. Then I take my hands and push it in and up a bit to see what it would look like if I had a nose job. At this point I'm really wishing I had a nose job and can't believe I never got one! After examining my nose from all the angles, I imagine I got a horrible nose job, like the kind that looks like a two-car garage. Then I decide maybe I'm better off the way it is. I go through this process a couple times a week—should I fix my nose or shouldn't I, should I or shouldn't I?"

Unfortunately, a lot of people spend time alone obsessing about supposed shortcomings in their looks, whether a receding hairline or a bulging waistline. It is as if any blemish or fault on the outside is equated with "spoiled goods," some imperfection that we feel we are hiding on the inside—the part of us that feels ugly, stupid, phoney, inadequate, or uncertain. Indeed, an inordinate amount of private time spent grooming, inspecting, and judging our physical appearance may be an unconscious or symbolic way of shoring up the external side of a damaged self—which is readily visible to others.

## NATURAL BODY FUNCTIONS

If most people are self-conscious about some aspect of their appearance, practically everyone experiences some discomfort even in *talking about* natural body functions in public.

In fact, such behaviors are usually brought up only in the context of a joke, at which it is permissible to laugh (but not too loudly).

Whereas in all human societies eating and drinking occur in the presence of others, excretion always takes place in private. Indeed, when dealing with any bodily fluids, people across cultures prefer being alone. This sanctuary of privacy has arisen not only for sanitary reasons (to separate waste products from living quarters), but to protect our dignity and safety when we are immobilized or helpless. Even when sneezing, we close our eyes, turn away, and cover our face with a cloth or hand, not only to avoid spreading germs, but also to afford some momentary privacy.

*Bathroom behaviors.* In his book on shame and privacy, Carl Schneider explains why elimination functions are universally restricted to the private sphere. First of all, the products of excretion are normally associated with decay. The smell and appearance that we find so offensive are nature's ways of reminding us to keep these functions separate from living quarters.

Beyond the simple concern for hygiene, there is a natural avoidant reaction toward elimination, as if it were the embodiment of evil. As is so often true with human conceptions of nature, there is a polarity associated with the body, a dichotomy between what is "good" (the heart, the spirit, the brain) and what is "bad" (the genitals or any body product).

Everyone has private patterns of bathroom behavior. Some people treat the elimination of bodily waste as a daily task that must be completed quickly, while others treat it as an opportunity for uninterrupted peace and quiet, a time alone to relax, think random thoughts, work out problems, or read. In fact, bathroom reading is one of those universals of private moments that many people engage in but few people ever discuss. Some people are quite particular in selecting reading material. One man is especially thoughtful about his choices:

"I've noticed I have an easier time on the toilet if I have something to read. It takes me a while to go to the bathroom in the morning, maybe twenty minutes. That's a long time to be sitting around staring at the towel rack.

"For me, the object is to find something that can be read in fifteen-minute intervals without having to spend time backtracking what you read previously. Ideally, it is best to find a book or magazine that presents a single idea you can mull over during the rest of the day. For a long time I was convinced that short stories were perfect for the bathroom as they are designed to be read in a single sitting. Now I feel I have a lot more freedom with a novel by Joyce or Proust since it doesn't matter where I start or leave off."

There is another aspect of private bathroom behavior that is universally experienced but rarely discussed. To the young, who are often able to go for twelve hours at a time without nature calling, urination is an occasional inconvenience. This childhood "annoyance" turns into a more common occupation in later adulthood as the bladder's capacity to store fluid decreases. A man in his forties describes the nocturnal annoyance of declining bladder functions:

"One of the most devastating signs that I was getting older was when I couldn't any longer make it through the night without having to get up and go to the bathroom. It seemed to happen all at once. Now, two, sometimes three times every night I get up in the middle of the night and stumble around trying to make it to the bathroom without running into a wall. See, the key is to do it without fully waking up, or then you can't get back to sleep. I shuffle along with my hands out in front of me so I don't run into a door or something. Then, when I get to the toilet, I lean against the wall so I don't sway too much. Women have it made—they can sit down—but guys have to stand there in the dark trying to concentrate on their aim and trying not to wake up. Sometimes I dribble on the floor or get my foot wet. If I try to find a towel, I'll wake up for sure, so I sort of drag my foot along the carpeting on the way back to bed."

*The private life of women.*   Although the menstrual period is a regular part of each woman's life cycle, this activity is rarely spoken about except in euphemisms like "it's that time of the month." Menstruation is a time that calls for extra self-nurturing efforts, a time when a woman feels permission to take special care of herself, both physically and emotionally. It is a time of vulnerability, when thresholds for tolerating frustration, stress, and deprivation are reduced. For many, it is accompanied by an assortment of uncomfortable symptoms including cramps, nausea, fatigue, tension, and irritability. Women also have a feeling of greater isolation during this time.

Anthropologist Peter Farb describes some of the superstitions that arose as menstruation was pushed behind closed doors:

> The superstitious caution against walking under ladders probably is a carryover from a time when people would not walk under bridges, trees, or cliffs if a menstruating female was about, lest some of her blood fall on them. In many societies, menstruating females are prohibited from touching objects of value and are blamed for accidents and the destruction of property.

Farb further cites the Roman writer Pliny the Elder as an example of the extreme positions that have been taken throughout history to isolate women during their menstrual cycle. Pliny believed that contact with menstrual blood "turns new wine sour, crops touched by it become barren, grafts die, seeds in gardens are dried up, the fruit of trees falls off, the edge of steel and the gleam of ivory are dulled, hives of bees die, even bronze and iron are at once seized by rust. . . ."

With legends like this circulating through the ages, it is no wonder there are still remnants of shame associated with menstruation. Representative of the feelings many women experience about their periods is the following disclosure:

"When I feel my period coming on I just want to crawl into bed and stay there until it's over. I don't like losing control over myself, becoming moody, crying more easily. As soon as my husband finds out it's that time of the month, he uses it as an excuse to downplay the significance of anything I might say—it's like I'm not taken seriously or the things I feel don't really count."

The specific way in which a woman takes care of herself during menstruation depends on more than her tolerance for physical discomfort. It is not surprising that the woman above feels she is not taken seriously by her husband during her period; she doesn't take herself seriously either. She has come to believe that one week per month is a complete waste—she feels helpless to control any aspect of her emotional life.

Yet even women who experience severe symptoms of premenstrual syndrome have learned to teach themselves and their spouses *not* to discount them during their difficult times. Instead they insist they be shown the same compassion and understanding they would offer to their husbands when the men are not feeling in top shape. Further, they try to adopt a more positive attitude in which menstruation is not viewed as "the Curse"; rather it is seen as a symbol of fertility, youth, and a natural hormonal cycle that encourages self-care and nurturance.

Of course, the cycles of men are not so clearly demarcated by a specific time of the month; men's biological cycles are ruled by hormonal pressures of a different nature. From the first wet dream of adolescence, males learn that the need to ejaculate every few hours, days, or weeks (depending on age and sex drive) is a wonderful yet seemingly uncontrolled drive that must be kept private.

## SELF-PLEASURING

For both men and women, this topic epitomizes one of the first things people think about when the topic of private moments is mentioned. Why is it so difficult for us to talk about masturbation? It is an activity practiced on a regular basis by 80 to 90 percent of the adult population. Yet there is strong disapproval in almost every culture. Throughout all recorded history, humans have been actively discouraged from masturbating for fear that the birth rate would decline because of reduced copulation. To reinforce the prohibition against masturbation, and to instill guilt in this supposed crime against humanity, medical and religious authorities have claimed (until relatively recently) that autoeroticism causes blindness, epilepsy, insanity, feeblemindedness, rheumatism, hemorrhoids, constipation, homosexuality, gonorrhea, stunted growth, and even death.

Although no physical or psychological harm is known to result from this activity unless it is done excessively, there is still a feeling that it is shameful and dirty. Even today, when we ought to know better, many people believe masturbation is somehow perverse. Generations of adolescents have retreated behind the locked door to test the strange new pleasures their genitals could bring them. As a result of the negative programming surrounding masturbation, these furtive journeys of self-discovery produce tremendous guilt and shame even when immortalized with humor in Phillip Roth's *Portnoy's Complaint*. Portnoy confesses to his therapist:

> I tear off my pants, furiously I grasp that battered battering ram to freedom, my adolescent cock, even as my mother begins to call from the other side of the bathroom. . . . Doctor, do you understand what I was up against? My wang was all I really had that I could call my own. . . . Oh my secrets, my shame, my palpitations, my flushes, my sweats! . . . Doctor, I can't stand any more being frightened like this over nothing! Bless me with manhood! Make me brave! Make me

strong! Make me whole! Enough of publically pleasing my parents while privately pulling my putz!

From a psychophysical standpoint rather than a religious one, masturbation is natural, normal, and self-nurturing. It is hardly a private crime against society; rather it is erotic fun that provides a lovely escape into pleasure. Indeed, there are a number of benefits to masturbation, as described by prominent sexologist Albert Ellis:

*Releasing tension.* Carolyn is an unemployed professional who has been feeling tremendous stress adjusting to the loss of her job. She especially does not like being in a position in which other people are making decisions that affect her life. While she despises the process of searching and interviewing for jobs, she is determined to stick with it. But sometimes the pressure becomes too much, and she finds her sleep disturbed, her moods jittery, and she has trouble concentrating. Even her usual relaxation strategies, hot baths and long walks, don't work all that well. For Carolyn, masturbation is the only thing that consistently reduces her stress:

"Every once in a while, I become aware of tension that I feel building up inside me, tension that can't seem to be released in any other way except by masturbating. It doesn't seem to have anything to do with how much sex I've been having, or how little sex I've been having. I just feel this pressure that won't go away. Nothing seems to work for me.

"I go through this internal dialogue, trying to reassure myself that everything will work out in the long run, if in the short run I can just calm down. I tell myself that it doesn't mean I don't enjoy sex with my husband just because occasionally I feel the need to do it myself. It really doesn't even feel like sex, but more like that feeling you get when you have to sneeze and it just won't come. And then when it does, you feel so much better.

"Usually, I lie down in bed and use a vibrator. It's not exactly a pleasurable experience. The sensations are too intense, so I try to distract myself so I can go with what's happening and relax. Afterward, I feel like a need has been taken care of and I can go back to whatever I was doing before."

*Increasing sexual responsiveness.* During masturbation you teach yourself to be more sexually responsive. In sex therapy, couples who are experiencing such sexual dysfunctions as premature ejaculation or orgasmic problems are encouraged to practice self-stimulation. They are urged to find the optimal approach by masturbating first in private, and then in front of their partners, to overcome inhibitions about their bodies as well as to improve communication. One woman who recently underwent treatment for sexual problems in her marriage reported the enormous benefits she discovered when masturbation was suggested as part of her therapy:

"I think the hardest part of my treatment in sex therapy was learning to become comfortable touching myself. It was kind of weird following assignments like trying a vibrator or a water massage, but first I had to be able to give myself orgasms before I could teach my husband to do it. Initially, it was so embarrassing to masturbate in front of my husband like I was supposed to. But that's what it took for me to finally have orgasms during intercourse."

*Promoting independence.* People without partners can seek sexual pleasure without encountering the risks of being dependent on others. Many single people find it humiliating having to resort to playing social games just to find sexual release for an evening. Legitimately, they fear the consequences of sex with an unknown partner. In addition to the risks of being assaulted or exposed to AIDS or venereal disease, they encounter the dangers inherent in becoming intimate with someone they hardly know—vulnerability, betrayal of trust, and rejection.

A single woman in her mid-fifties describes the sense of independence that masturbation gives her:

"I've been single for a long time. I would love to be in a relationship with somebody, but years ago I reconciled myself that it just isn't in the stars. I'm a happy person—I like my life. But sex isn't part of the picture—at least not with a partner. So I masturbate frequently. It helps me sleep. I crawl into bed with a sexy book that slowly turns me on and then I sort of just work myself into it."

*Balancing sex drives.* Masturbation provides a means of balancing the different sexual needs inherent in marital relationships. Because of differences in age, experience, and hormonal systems, it is rare for partners to share identical preferences in the quality and quantity of their sex lives. Whereas one spouse might like sex every day, or even twice a day, the other may be quite satisfied with an orgasm once a month. While the discrepancy between partners is usually not that wide, most people must negotiate with their spouses over the frequency with which they have sex.

Masturbation becomes the equalizer, allowing one partner to occasionally (or regularly) take care of sexual needs while placing fewer demands on the mate. This is done without resorting to extramarital affairs that could destabilize the relationship. One young woman, whose husband travels a great deal because of business obligations, uses masturbation as a safe outlet for sexual needs that might otherwise lead to having affairs:

"Gosh, if I didn't do it to myself I would probably have to have an affair or something. What I like to do is to lie in the sun nude in our backyard. I slowly rub oil all over and let my body heat up. Then I take ice cubes and place them on the most sensitive places. It's a major turn-on to know that anyone could catch me at any moment. In fact, I pretend I am preparing myself as a gift for someone who will make love to me. Sometimes, I get so into the fantasy that I put on a sexy teddy, do up my hair and makeup, and then lie down and masturbate for an hour or more. Then I drift off to heaven."

The woman who told the preceding story is a mother and housewife who is much admired for her well-organized household and meticulous appearance. She has never had another sexual partner besides her husband of ten years. She feels close to her mate and communicates quite openly about all things—except the sexual fantasies she acts out when she is alone.

By the time her husband returns from work, she has slipped back into her clothes and her role as dutiful and loving wife. As far as anyone else would ever know, she spent her day cleaning the house, running errands, and cooking dinner. This aspect of her secret self remains safely shut away behind her innocent demeanor.

There is no end to what the imagination can devise for self-pleasure. These private moments lead to the discovery of increasingly more intense pleasures and provide the variation in sexual activity that many people crave. My interviews were full of accounts of those who have used vibrators, pillows, underwear, and various inanimate objects as aids to self-stimulation. One enterprising woman rewarded herself after the laundry was done by sitting on the washing machine when it was on the spin cycle!

It is apparent from these voices—men and women, single and married, old and young—that there are an infinite number of ways to reach orgasm by self-stimulation. Yet, masturbation cannot replace the special kind of emotional, spiritual, and physical closeness that can only be experienced with a partner. Masturbation is a solitary act, a private activity that best exemplifies the heights of ecstasy that are possible when alone. It does not threaten relationships with others, but rather enhances the quality of time spent with yourself. The more sensuous, sensitive, and skilled you can be during self-stimulation, the more responsive a lover you can be with your mate. Masturbation teaches you to better appreciate your own body and what it is capable of. It is one of the most effective ways to nurture yourself and release stress.

## REDUCING STRESS THROUGH RELAXATION

The opposite of heightened excitement as a form of self-nurturance is reduced stimulation in the form of relaxation. After a strenuous period of work or creative thought, we all require time out to allow our minds to rest and our bodies to recover. Settled into a comfortable chair, you can easily pass a few hours or an evening indulging in a favorite method of relaxation—taking a nap, meditating, eating a favorite snack food, watching television, reading, listening to music, knitting. Or you can unwind with a physical activity like washing the car or going for a walk in the woods. This is time for decompressing, shutting down in order to nurture yourself and build up energy reserves. These activities are chosen because they permit you to "check out" temporarily from the usual strains and routines of daily existence. They give your brain and body a chance to recover and recuperate.

Consider, for example, the experience of one busy professional who enjoys the relaxing challenge of assembling puzzles:

"I love to work jigsaw puzzles when I'm alone. I couldn't care less what the picture is. When I buy them I look for those that are the most complicated and difficult, but I don't like them to be totally one color. Any of the ones that are about two thousand pieces allow me to work on them without having to think about what I'm doing. The world goes away. I became one with that puzzle. If there was somebody else in the room I would have no idea they are there. It's not totally unlike what I experienced when I used to meditate. It requires enough concentration to keep me focused, but not so much that I can't be two places at the same time. There's almost nothing that's as relaxing for me.

"When I sit down at the table I feel so excited—I have this awareness that I'm about to enter a world that's all mine. Everything else is going to go away. Initially, there's a moment of estrangement when I first sit down. I haven't worked on this puzzle for a day or two. It's been sitting on this table. The pieces are still where I left them. They're not my friends at this moment. There's this strange reacquainting of learning why I put certain pieces where they are, the various nuances of shades of blue if I'm doing a sky. Slowly I get back into the throes of becoming lost again, but I'm not fully conscious of when that moment occurs."

Others find the greatest relaxation in a book or a favorite radio or TV program. After a long day, an hour or two of television may be a valuable opportunity to forget your own worries. One man explains the benefits he feels from watching TV:

"When I've had a hard day one of the first things I like to do is turn on the 'animal channel'—that cable station, Public Broadcasting or something, that's always showing nature programs. I've had this tough day of feeling like I'm being eaten alive, and then I see this gorgeous gazelle flying through the air until it is snatched by a leopard that proceeds to devour it while it is still kicking. I watch that on TV and think, hey, I don't have it so bad."

Another advantage of watching television or listening to the radio is that you can combine it with other activities that don't require your full attention. A fifty-six-year-old college professor describes how he relaxes when the rest of the household is asleep and his work is done:

"I love cable, those fifty-six channels you flip through. I look for a sporting event—baseball, basketball, tennis, even water polo. I don't care. I'm mesmerized. It's live. It's real.

It's happening right now. It's not being acted. Usually I'll watch for an hour or so, then I putter around some more. I have these lists of things to do. I water the plants. I like to get stuff done. Then back to the TV and that wonderful remote-control device that allows me to live a thousand lives in an hour."

Others spend hours absorbed in operating a personal computer. As long as you are careful to maintain a healthy balance between the time you spend watching television or playing with a computer and the time you spend in more active pursuits, you have little to be concerned about. Passive forms of solitary entertainment provide life experiences in a diluted form where you are an observer rather than an active participant. It is certainly true there is no substitute for travel and real-life involvement. On the other hand, how else in a single hour could you watch the birth of a snow leopard, a world figure skating competition, and a one-act play?

Such spectator events have a long and illustrious history, from the Colosseum and Globe Theatre to Yankee Stadium and Rockefeller Center. Throughout history, humans have sought forums in which they can encounter situations vicariously that they wouldn't ordinarily be able to experience. This broadens and enriches our perspective, as well as permitting us to release unexpressed emotions. When used judiciously—not to avoid life but to educate and entertain, to provide periods of rejuvenation—various forms of relaxation offer wonderful stimulation, fun, and growth. This is as true for the relatively passive forms of self-nurturance just mentioned as for those that involve getting out into the natural world.

## COMMUNING WITH NATURE

Relaxing at home is something we do on a daily basis; for special occasions we require a different setting in order to gain a fresh perspective. One of the themes that runs throughout the pattern of solitary moments in people's lives is the periodic need to take time out to center oneself, preferably in a locale that offers maximum seclusion.

The world of Nature is ideally suited for being alone. Trees, foliage, water, hills, and valleys provide protection from intrusions. There are vast expanses of scenery to view, woods to walk through, mountains to climb, lakes to swim, and meadows to sit in. The sounds of Nature—crickets, coyotes, birds, rustling leaves, rushing water—excite, soothe, and entertain.

People feel drawn to wilderness areas, parks, and other natural settings in order to get away from societal rules and laws, artificial structures like fences, buildings, stop signs, and billboards, not to mention the surveillance of friends, family, and neighbors. Those I interviewed reported several other reasons why they prefer to relax in natural settings:

*Peace and tranquility.* The sights, sounds, and sensations of Nature are intrinsically relaxing—the warmth of the sun, the sounds of rushing water, the beauty of a quiet lake, mountain peak, or forest. One busy mother of three described the peaceful feelings she experiences while alone in the woods:

"I like to go camping with my family. But because I have three sons, things can seem pretty frantic, even in the woods. Nevertheless, I always find time to go for long, slow walks by myself. I can feel the earth below my feet, so springy and soft. There's a coolness in the air and closeness to the trees. It's so comforting, I never want to leave it."

*Meditative self-renewal.* In the quiet of a hillside, wooded path, or mountaintop, it is easier to hear yourself think. Many people I spoke to reported that one of the primary benefits of spending time alone in Nature is that they are able to attain a state of real mental clarity.

Here is an excerpt from the journal kept by a man who recorded his thoughts during a solo cross-country ski trip in the Colorado Rockies:

"This is exactly what I have worked so hard for—uninterrupted hours upon hours to sit alone, think, feel, see. I am in my own meadow, not another inhabitant within earshot in any direction. On one side there is a gradually rising wall of peaks. The other side is bordered by a stand of evergreens.

"I sit underneath a large tree with views of either side to my left or right. The sun is absolutely intense. Even stripped down to my long underwear I feel warmed. The snow sparkles around me, crusted and untrampled as far as I can see, except for my own tracks leading into this valley. It seems like I have waited my whole life for these precious hours. Nothing else exists except the feel of the wind and the sound of one bird who watches me watching him."

*Nature study.*   Nature represents a limitless opportunity for learning about the mysteries of life. One woman feels drawn to nature because she can experience a deeper level of herself as a human being as she feels connected to all the living things around her:

"When I'm walking in the woods sometimes I feel drawn to certain trees. I go up to them and hug them; it feels like an energy connection, like I draw strength from them. As I walk along I talk to little bushes and herbs, asking them: 'If I picked you and took you home and dried you, what are you good for?' And I always talk to animals—well, I'm careful with skunks—but raccoons and squirrels. I don't say words to them; I talk to them with my eyes: 'I'm really glad I ran into you and you let me spend time with you. Be careful, because there are other two-leggeds around here that might hurt you.'"

For those people who can't escape into the wilderness, patios, decks, backyards, and parks can provide privacy and a natural setting for relaxation and contemplation. From any of these vantage points you can take some sun and watch birds or squirrels. Even standing in the rain or snow can be relaxing, as one urban dweller describes: "I love the magic of a windless winter night when heavy snow is fall- ing—those nights that aren't too cold—you can almost *hear* the snow as big, wet pieces cover everything and transform it into a sparkling icy kingdom."

*Gardening.*   Another common way that people experi- ence self-renewal in the natural world is by gardening. A teacher relates the special joy she feels working on her lawn because she can immediately see the results of her labors, unlike the barely noticeable changes that occur in her stu- dents over the course of a year:

"An activity I enjoy doing when the temperature is right is weeding my lawn. This is one thing that I do that no one disturbs. No one wants to join in. And if I'm in a secluded area, no one can find me. It's very relaxing. I just focus in on the task at hand—challenged by seeing how long a root I can pull out of the earth. When I'm done, I can look over a patch of grass and know that I made a difference in making it look better."

*The challenge of adventure.*   Not all experiences of nature are passive ones. Some people hunger for the oppor- tunity to use the natural world as a way to challenge them- selves. People undertake hazardous solitary adventures for the dual test of exploring new territory both without and within. Certainly climbing a peak, or sailing a ship around the world solo, requires great physical stamina and courage; yet such activities also involve tremendous inner resolve. These adventurers are exploring not only new territory of the world, but also new areas of themselves.

Tom Neale spent five years alone on an uninhabited island purely for the challenge of surviving on his own. He encountered a number of physical dangers, including sickness and storms. But his most difficult times were spent struggling not with the weather but with his thoughts and feelings. He had a particularly difficult time adjusting to his own internal rhythms after a lifetime of conforming to those of his culture. After returning to civilization, he reflected on his experience:

> Now that I had six years to relive every moment I had spent on the island, and to reflect on the mistakes I had made, I rather ruefully came to the conclusion that I, who loved the leisurely pace of life on the islands, had failed when I reached Suvarov the first time to put into practice the lessons learned during half a lifetime in the South Pacific. I could understand how it happened. I had been so proud of my island that I wanted to do everything in a rush. And so, in a curiously ironic way, I had unwittingly imposed on the timeless quality of the island the speed and bustle of modern cities from which I had been so anxious to escape.

Neale kept himself moving at such a frantic pace—building shelter, finding food, protecting himself against the elements—that he rarely gave himself the chance to relax and simply be with himself. He had escaped the routine of the average urban man who distracts himself with productive pursuits to avoid confronting the self, only to end up doing the same thing. He believed his greatest accomplishment was not his survival, but rather the depths to which he was eventually able to explore his soul and spirit. After realizing that in his escape from society he had also escaped himself, Neale returned to his island ten years later to live out the rest of his life.

In Neale's solitary island life, the task of enjoying his own company became his greatest challenge. It was no accident that he and other explorers, such as Admiral Richard Byrd, or Joshua Slocum (mentioned in a previous chapter), set out on their journeys alone. Certainly things would have been easier for them with others along to provide company and to share the work. But the purpose of such expeditions is not to explore the outside world only, but the world within—to learn how you react under stress with nobody else to depend upon; to take sufficient time in isolated space to get to know yourself more fully; to come to terms with exactly who you are and what you are doing here on Earth.

*Freedom to be natural.* Nature is, by definition, a relaxed, natural environment, one that allows us to reduce inhibitions and social conventions. The very setting beckons us to revert to the ways of our ancestors. In the woods we stalk prey; we hunt and fish; our walk becomes lighter and more carefree. Alone in the woods, we feel more free to be our most natural selves. This feeling is described by one man in the following unusual experience:

"I was once in a remote forest when I was living in Europe. Everything was lush and green. The ground was springy and soft. The trees were thick. And everything smelled like . . . like only a forest can smell. I spent the day walking around, exploring the flora and fauna, following a stream to see where it led, trying to catch a glimpse of the wildlife. It was one of the most magical days of my life. I had never felt so peaceful and calm. I fell in love with the world, and with this special forest. Without quite thinking about what I was doing, I fell to the soft ground and embraced the earth, my body moving as if I was making love to the forest. It was my way of consummating the love affair I had that day with Nature."

These solo experiences of traveling in Nature do not necessarily promote further isolation. Instead, they can facilitate a closer connection to others, just as they help you to focus your concentration on something outside of yourself. When you feel connected to the natural world, you also feel a greater affinity for the rest of the human race.

The paradox of solitude is that *private* moments enhance *public* effectiveness. By taking care of yourself and meeting your personal needs for time alone to relax and decompress, you are in a much better position to respond to others' demands. When you improve the quality of your self-nurturing activities by making time for a walk in the woods, a hot bath, a compelling novel or movie, you feel better about yourself and become less resentful of other obligations. You feel better prepared to take care of the daily business of life.

CHAPTER

# 6

# *Being Self-Directed*

$S$OLITUDE PRESENTS IDEAL circumstances for
being productive and reflective, allowing focused concentration without external distractions or pressures. You have
maximum freedom to do what you wish, whenever and however you prefer. Yet in order to make the most of private time,
you need a certain degree of motivation, self-discipline,
and self-direction to initiate tasks and then follow them
through. This is true of any activity in which people engage
to improve the quality of their lives in some way—studying
a new subject, writing in a journal, or staying with a physical exercise or meditation regimen.

## USING SOLITUDE PRODUCTIVELY

People who are most satisfied and comfortable with their
time alone are those who feel productive during their private moments. They feel a sense of accomplishment in how
they spend that time—tinkering on a car engine, crocheting
an afghan, reading a good book—any activity that makes
them feel they are learning, growing, or making progress.

The ability to convert even extreme solitude into something meaningful is the principal task of anyone who is
interested in enhancing the quality of time spent alone. This
is as true for a person living alone after divorce or widowhood as it is for a prisoner in solitary confinement. Cut off
from all stimulation and contact, prisoners of war are forced
to create their own internal methods of dealing with the ultimately monotonous existence. Time is the principal enemy.

114

Jacob Timmerman was a Jewish publisher in Argentina during that country's oppressive regime of the 1970s. He survived years of languishing in a solitary cell and was able to share how he dealt with the torture of isolation. His courage, determination, and patience demonstrate the power of the human spirit to be productive even in the most extreme environments of deprivation:

> Long afterwards, I realized that I had developed a withdrawal technique. I tried through every available means, while inside my solitary cell, during interrogations, long torture sessions, and after sessions, when only time remained, all of time, time on all sides and in every cranny of the cell, time suspended on the walls, on the ground, in my hands, only time, I tried to maintain some professional activity disconnected from the events around me or that I imagined to be going on around me. Deliberately I evaded conjecture on my own destiny, that of my family and the nation. I devoted myself simply to being consciously a solitary man entrusted with a specific task.

Productive activities, or the illusion of accomplishment, is what gives meaning to the prisoner's solitary existence. Whether inventing some device, practicing push-ups, working out complex mathematical equations, recalling the names of baseball players, plotting a novel, or Timmerman's favorite activity—stocking an imaginary bookstore with the world's greatest literature—the inmate marks time by what he has done.

Solitude is not a prison term but an opportunity to channel concentration and energy in a singular direction, free of all external distractions. Therefore, one way to improve the quality of your private time is to add creative and productive activities. Chief among self-directed activities are those involving efforts to know your inner self better. Artistic pursuits and hobbies often enable you to learn more about your capabilities at the same time you are constructing a project. Even more facilitative is an examination of your life by regularly reflecting and writing in a journal.

## KEEPING A PERSONAL JOURNAL

One unique feature of journal writing is its complete secrecy. Knowing it will forever remain for your eyes only (except for parts you may occasionally share with others) allows you to transcend shame, criticism, and approval, and feel completely free to write whatever you think.

It is also through communication with yourself that you can work through the negative associations of being alone. The journal is a place for self-therapy that can accomplish many of the same goals as work with a professional, especially if it is used at regular intervals. As with any learning effort, daily practice is preferable. Writing in a journal can improve your self-discipline, analytic ability, and self-counseling skills, among many other useful functions.

Anaïs Nin, a writer who kept a journal throughout most of her life, produced over 150,000 pages of self-reflections and descriptions of her friends and acquaintances, who were among the most famous thinkers of her day. She believed the process of journaling represents the ultimate appreciation of private moments. She found the activity to be extremely useful as "an exercise in creative will; as an exercise in synthesis; as a means to create a world according to our wishes, not those of others; as a means of creating the self, of giving birth to ourselves."

Like Nin, other writers and thinkers throughout history have discovered that reflecting in a journal on a regular basis does much more than help them organize their work in process. It enhances one's inner life in a number of other ways:

*Working through internal conflicts.* Writing is, by its very nature, an activity that encourages introspection because it records what is going on inside—how you think and feel, and how you perceive the world. As such, it is particularly well suited to personal problem solving, since in the process of describing what is happening you will often come up with ideas for what needs to be done. Even when you fail to come up with any immediate solutions, journaling seems to help define the nature of the conflict. Once you've labeled the situation, you can return to it again and again as you describe the parameters, share the frustration, list failed efforts, and sometimes do no more than simply own up to your confusion.

Professional writers have always favored the journal as a private place to work on personal issues, including working through blocks to their productivity. John Steinbeck, for example, used a journal to prime himself each day before he continued work on his great novel *East of Eden*. Feeling blocked and uncertain as to how the characters would evolve and the plot unfold, Steinbeck described himself as sitting forlornly at his new marble writing table, staring at his collection of freshly sharpened Mongol $2^3/8$ F pencils. He used his journal as a way to work through the fears and apprehensions that were getting in the way of his creativity.

> February 13 (Tuesday)
> It must be told that my second work day is a bust as far as getting into the writing. I suffer as always from the fear of putting down the first line. It is amazing the terrors, the magic, the prayers, the straightening shyness that assails one. It is as though the words were not only indelible but that they spread out like dye in water and color everything around them. A strange and mystic business writing. The Book of the Dead is as good and as highly developed as anything in the 20th century and much better than most. And yet in spite of this lack of a continuing excellence hundreds of thousands of people are in my shoes—praying feverishly for relief from their word pangs.

For professional writers like Steinbeck, or anyone else who can express himself on paper, journaling provides a way to unload pent-up feelings and thereby neutralize their power to block further progress. The goal is not necessarily to fix a particular problem or resolve an issue once and for all, but simply to explore fully and describe completely the exact nature of what you are feeling, thinking, and experiencing.

*Systematic problem solving.* As a task in itself, writing down your innermost conflicts and confusions is cathartic. However, there is something to be said for attempting to work things out in systematic, step-by-step fashion. Those who are more goal- than process-oriented are not content to merely write down what is going on—they are driven to resolve the struggle. They can benefit from problem-solving strategies that can help them be as precise and methodical as possible.

People who are stymied in some major decision—which job to take, whether to follow a particular course of action, whether to get married, whether to have children—often profit from writing their thoughts down on paper, in what Ben Franklin called "moral algebra" for decision making. In one detailed problem-solving strategy developed by educator Robert Carkhuff, the journal writer tries to avoid some of the more common pitfalls that can mar thinking processes. These include exaggerating the importance of a decision, believing there is a single right answer, fearing that you will make a mistake, and not wanting responsibility for the outcome.

Here are the sequential steps suggested in a systematic problem-solving approach:

First, you need to thoroughly explore the internal conflict, paying particular attention to how it developed, the ways it is manifested, and your feelings and thoughts on the matter.

For example, Noelle is feeling overwhelmed by all the demands of her life—children to care for, a house to maintain, a husband to respond to, friends who want her atten-

tion, books sitting unread on her nightstand, plus the demands of an interesting but very draining profession that
occupies forty-five hours per week. She feels frustrated, exhausted, and trapped. She is able to get in touch with many
of these feelings by writing them down.

Next, develop some insight as to how things ended up
the way they have.

Continuing our example, over the course of several journal entries Noelle realizes that she has become someone she
doesn't much like: driven, compulsive, overscheduled, short-
tempered, with little time to be alone. She finds herself
resenting her family, avoiding her friends, hiding out at
work where at least she is paid in tangible terms for her
efforts. She notes the amount of time she has spent fantasizing about ways she wants to spend her money—a new
house, a new car, a trip to Spain. She also notes that she may
be living up to expectations that are not her own. She
writes out the voices she hears inside her head—of her
mother telling her she's awful for neglecting her family, and
the determination Noelle feels to prove her wrong, to do it
all and do it perfectly. She sees on paper the expectations of
her children, husband, parents, boss, friends, and realizes it
is futile to keep things going the way they are. Something
has to give.

Once you have examined the history of the problem, the
next step is to break things down into more specific, behavioral elements that can be worked on.

Noelle realizes that the requirements of her life exceed
the time available. She is overscheduled beyond the point
where she could ever catch up. She has been unable to set
limits regarding what she can comfortably handle. She feels
the only possible solution is to cut back some of her activities and change her lifestyle in some significant way. But
how can she decide what must go?

Consider all possible courses of action. Avoid criticizing
and censoring yourself. Instead, just list on paper all the
options that may be helpful.

Noelle creates a list of more than thirty-five ideas, including soliciting more help (from her husband, a housekeeper, a babysitter, an assistant at work), replacing certain activities (cutting back her hours at work, attending fewer professional or civic meetings), and negotiating more time for herself. Through her journal, eventually Noelle reaches a point where she has clarified the source of her problems, identified what she can do to rectify them, and has developed ideas on how to put the plan into action.

This method suggested by Carkhuff, or any other form of written self-analysis, trains you to spend a portion of your private time organizing your ideas and gaining a more objective perspective of some aspect of your life. You are thus able to identify more clearly the feelings, thoughts, goals, and behaviors that are of greatest priority to you, and to target your efforts toward reaching those objectives.

*Noting perceptions of the world.*  With a journal as a lifelong companion, you can become a more astute observer of the human condition. You develop a sensitivity to detail in others' behavior, enabling you to become an applied sociologist, looking at the events around you with an educated eye.

The poet Rainer Maria Rilke created, over a seven-year period, the notebooks of a fictional character, one who used the full spectrum of possibilities in journal writing. In the entry below, the character processes insights about the world around him:

I sit here reading a poet. There are a lot of people in the reading-room; but one is not aware of them. They are in the books. Sometimes they move in the pages, like sleepers who turn over between two dreams. Ah, how good it is to be among reading people. Why are they not always like that? You can go up to one of them and touch him lightly; he feels nothing. And if in rising, you chance to bump lightly against a neighbor and excuse yourself, he nods toward the side from which he hears your voice, his face turns toward you and does not see you, and his hair is like that of a man asleep. How comforting that is. And I sit and have a poet.

Life experience has trained you to form observations about human nature, about the world and how it works. You have a personal philosophy and a set of values that are uniquely your own. Since no one sees the world the same way you do, your individual window permits you to write your own unique perceptions about what you sense, see, hear, and feel.

*Important remembrances.* Perhaps of all the functions the diary has served throughout history, its greatest value has been as a repository for noting significant events. The adolescent records her first kiss, her first date, her first defeats and the accompanying feelings of elation or despair. As you grow older you can describe other major transitions—graduations, marriage, childbirth, the death of loved ones. In years that follow you can go back to any previous time and relive what occurred and how you felt.

The novelist Albert Camus struggled throughout most of his life with issues of loneliness and alienation, themes that played themselves out in many of his books. Like so many writers, the seeds for many of his philosophical ideas and literary plots came from personal experiences that were often recorded in the notebooks he kept since he was a young man. One especially impressionable event was noted in his journal during his mid-twenties:

*Paris*
The woman from the floor above has killed herself by jumping into the courtyard of the hotel. She was thirty-one, said one of the tenants. Old enough to live, and, since she had lived a little, to die. The shadow of the drama still lingers on in the hotel. She sometimes used to come down and ask the owner's wife to let her stay for supper. She suddenly used to kiss her—from a need to feel another person's warmth and

presence. It ended with a three-inch split in her forehead.
Before she died she said: "At last."

*Practicing new ways of being.* Writing in a journal
can also be a form of rehearsal for reality. Free of external
restraints and judgments, you are able to experiment with
alternative ways of thinking, feeling, acting, being. In this
private reflection you can assess areas of your life in need of
upgrading, or concerns and problems that require attention.
You can apply what writer May Sarton found so helpful in
her journals—honest self-scrutiny that leads to constructive
change:

> I woke in tears this morning. I wonder whether it is possible
> at nearly sixty to change oneself radically. Can I learn to
> control resentment and hostility, the ambivalence, born some-
> where far below the conscious level? If I cannot, I shall lose
> the person I love. There is nothing to be done but go ahead
> with life moment by moment and hour by hour—put out
> birdseed, tidy the rooms, try to create order and peace
> around me even if I cannot achieve it inside me. Now at ten
> thirty there is such radiant light outside the house feels dark.
> I look through the hall into the cozy room, all in darkness,
> right through to the window at the end, and a transparent
> sheaf of golden and green leaves. And here in my study the
> sunlight is that autumn white, so clear, it calls for an inward
> act to match it . . . clarify, clarify.

Tristine Rainer, a consultant who holds journaling work-
shops around the country, echoes the sentiments expressed
by Sarton and many other advocates of daily writing. In
summarizing what she has learned after teaching journal
writing for many years, Rainer comments on the am-
bivalence people feel in shielding the most intimate part of
themselves from others:

> Even if you never share a sentence of your diary with anyone
> else, you will share it through your life. Its existence will
> touch other people by the way it changes you and permits

you to develop in self-awareness, directness, and honesty. As you acquire and refine the talent for helping yourself in the diary, you will also grow in your ability to understand and nourish others. While it permits you to take responsibility for your own emotional well-being, it also opens the way for a deep understanding of human nature.

It is in the process of clarification that journaling, or any activity of solitary reflection, allows you to regain a sense of meaning in your life. You can work through struggles with loneliness and boredom; establish goals for the future; reveal thoughts and feelings; promote insights. Yet there are limits to self-understanding without new input and action. Journal writing and other solitary tools provide the impetus for life-altering events, especially when stimulated by the new learning and growth that come from sustained and disciplined study.

## SELF-DIRECTED STUDY

What journal writing can be to your emotional life, study can be to your intellectual stimulation. Both require a degree of self-discipline, and they complement each other in that they are interchangeable as input and output—that is, sometimes studying a subject is strengthened by personalizing it in your writing; and explorations in a journal may lead you to satisfy your curiosity in other areas. For example, I read about a character in a novel who exhibits the fascinating symptoms of multiple-personality disorder. I muse in my journal about the multiplicity of my own temperament and identify several distinct "people" who live inside me—the confident professional, the shy partygoer, the selfless altruist, the self-centered narcissist, the lazy sludge, the fearless truthseeker. It is the last part of me that wins out this time—I decide to make a study of multiplicity, devouring everything on the subject I can get my hands on.

This intellectual self-directed study once again leads me to personalize what I've learned in my journal. I write of my fears: What if I really am unstable inside? What if the negative parts of me become more dominant? How can I better access the parts of me that I like the most?

The interaction between input and output, between what you learn and how you apply it to your existence, is the basis for all life changes. Daniel has been addicted to change throughout most of his life. When he was in his twenties, he thought nothing of changing relationships, jobs, houses, friends, cars, anything to create new excitement. In his thirties, married with two children, Daniel could no longer follow his whims and uproot his life for new excitement so easily. Life became stale and predictable, and he felt ashamed of his complacency. Then he stumbled upon a way to satisfy his need for periodic stimulation without initiating drastic changes in his life:

"Studying has become for me, in my forties, a way that I can pursue change in my life, but without having to disrupt my external life. I will select some area that holds some fascination for me, or even one that I have always been apprehensive about, and I will devote a week, a month, even a year or two to learning everything I can about the subject. For example, I have always been afraid of math. I got lousy grades in high school and totally avoided it in college. Now, however, I have been devoting my spare time to mastering what I once was so afraid of. I started with algebra and trigonometry. And now I'm working my way through calculus.

"Before math, it was human anatomy. Before that, it was philosophy, Russian history, yoga, Spanish. It could be anything. But what is so interesting to me is that these studying projects that I undertake seem just as challenging and exciting to me as, once upon a time, I got such a thrill out of hitchhiking through Europe or moving to a new house. I've found that the changes that take place on the inside can be just as satisfying as those dramatic ones I used to initiate on the outside."

Self-directed study is indeed a productive way to create internal excitement and challenges in your life. It is among the most rewarding of solitary pursuits, since it requires lengthy periods of peace and quiet for focused concentration. And it allows you to satisfy your curiosity about what you long to understand.

Zoologist Desmond Morris describes his hunger as a child for time alone to study the things that interested him. He especially felt a curiosity to understand the workings of all living things. He spent hours collecting lizards, snakes, hedgehogs, mice, newts, toads, birds, and fish. But it was when he was given his first microscope that he plunged himself thoroughly into the private world of natural history:

> At the base of the microscope case there was a shallow drawer and in it I discovered some Victorian slides. I enjoyed looking at these under the lens, but it was living things I really wanted to study, so I set off on an urgent collecting trip. My grandmother owned a small lake and that was where I headed, jangling a suitable array of buckets, bottles, and jars to hold the slime, sludge, and weeds that I needed. Once there, I squelched about in the shadows like a diminutive water buffalo, scooping up strands and globules of unspeakable filth until all my containers were full. Triumphantly I returned to the gleaming microscope and began my impatiently awaited exploration into the microscopic world.
>
> I was shattered by what I saw. I felt I was entering a secret kingdom, where flagella undulated, cilia beat, cells divided, antennae twitched, and tiny organs pulsated. I spent so much time with my head bowed over the eyepiece of this magical instrument, and became so engrossed with what I saw, that I would cheerfully have dived down the tube of the microscope, like Alice down her rabbit hole.

In solitary study you devour new information for understanding yourself and the world around you. You take in new ideas that, in turn, help you to formulate your own opinions about why you act the way you do. Such learning not only helps increase your inner wisdom, but also builds

your confidence and self-esteem. You feel better about yourself when you have taken steps to keep yourself functioning
optimally. And this is true for your body as well as your
mind and spirit.

## SOLITARY EXERCISING

"Every chance I get, maybe three or four times per week, I
ride my bike. In the winter I have a wind trainer in the
basement to put my bike on. I put on my earphones, play
the radio real loud, turn out the lights, and pedal hard for
twenty or thirty minutes. After a few minutes I can hear my
heart pumping louder than the music. It's pitch-black—I'm
just pedaling away in the dark. Sometimes it almost feels
like I'm hallucinating. When the weather is nice, I go for
long rides outside. I go until it hurts—twenty, thirty, fifty
miles—depending on how much time I have. I never get
bored outside—there's too much to concentrate on. Let
your mind wander too far, you'll hit gravel or a pothole, and
that's that. There's a lot to keep me busy, switching gears,
planning my route, timing the stoplights so I don't have to
stop, keeping an eye on the speedometer, calculating my
average speed, keeping a steady cadence going, and watching for cars."

Just as this man finds his solitary bicycle jaunts invigorating, people discover their own personal preferences for
forms of exercise that provide mental relaxation as well as
physical conditioning. Whether you prefer rowing, weight
lifting, running, cross-country skiing, hiking, walking, or
swimming, you can use the private time inside your head in
different ways. Your mind will resort to several different
methods of occupying itself while you are working out, depending on such factors as your ability to focus concentration, your threshold level for boredom, the degree of stress
in your life, and the degree of comfort you feel in your own

company. You may recognize yourself in one of these four common styles of mental activity during exercise:

*The escapist* sees exercise as a necessary and unavoidable task that must be endured, like taking out the garbage or filing tax returns. It is not done for any intrinsic pleasure that might be experienced during the activity, but only for the desired result—burning off calories, firming up muscles, reducing tension. Wearing a dreamy-eyed look, this runner, bicyclist, or swimmer will be a thousand miles away reliving favorite fantasies to escape the physical pain or boredom of the exercise regime. As one runner puts it: "I hate running, actually. I just want to get it over with. I prefer to listen to my Walkman, but if the news is on, or I get bored with the music, I might switch it off and think about anything other that what I'm doing."

*The problem solver* sees the "downtime" during exercise as an opportunity for greater productivity. Inclined toward an ambitious and compulsive approach to life, he treats any time alone—in the bathroom, in the car, on an exercycle—as a chance to reflect on the day's schedule, planning agendas, finding solutions to nagging problems. One businessman who works fourteen-hour days remarked: "I always carry a small pencil and piece of paper with me in case I get an idea I want to remember. The hard part is writing while I'm walking."

*The competitor* displays a certain obsessiveness in the need to constantly improve performance. Such a person is constantly checking watch, pulse rate, breathing rhythm, body stress, and other factors to monitor progress toward personal goals of improved performance. One woman explained her point of view on the subject: "I've been keeping charts for years where I mark down all my times, distances, and how I felt during the run. When I'm actually on

the road I try to concentrate on the ways I've been coached.
I focus on a spot just ahead on the road. I have to work at
staying loose. I keep track of my times at various points."

*The meditator* approaches exercise as a time for enjoying and flowing with what is occurring. If you are a meditator, you are content to experience yourself completely in
your solitude. Your sense organs become exquisitely tuned
to the environment. Seeing, hearing, and feeling all occur
without conscious awareness. You move with rhythm and
grace, seemingly without effort. And you reach a meditative
trance state where pain, time, worries, other people, all vanish into the vortex, leaving only the sounds of your own
breathing.

One woman I interviewed described this state of complete immersion in which she enjoys the intrinsic pleasure
of using her body:

"I love to dance. Turn the music up real loud, close the
shades, and just let myself go. Sometimes I can dance for
hours until I fall from exhaustion. I warm up with slow
music—just swaying and floating. Then I might twirl
around like a ballerina to classical pieces I like. But the best
is loud rock and roll—on the radio if I don't feel like changing records. I dance and dance with the music, losing myself
totally in the process."

Any of these internal styles of exercising are potentially
beneficial (if not carried to excess) during the time spent in
solitary sweats. Whatever individual method is preferred,
those people who commit themselves to exercising alone on
a regular basis find their lives enriched in several ways:

*Enjoying the quiet time.* Solitary exercise gives people the opportunity to insulate themselves from the usual
pressures of daily existence. "I much prefer to run by myself because it gives me time to think. I plan the day that
lies ahead, and go over the previous one. Occasionally, on

Sundays, I run with a friend—and it's real different. I like the companionship, but I miss the time by myself. We end up talking about meaningless stuff just to make the time go faster. I end up focusing on my friend rather than myself; and I need time to be with myself."

*Avoiding having to compromise with others.* Exercising alone allows people to do what they want, when they want, for however long they prefer. "I have always enjoyed playing tennis but I hate having to depend on a partner. It's the same thing at work—everything I do depends on waiting for somebody else to do what they are supposed to do. But I can run whenever I want to, for as long as I want to, wherever I want to go. I don't have to negotiate or compromise with anyone. I can do exactly what I want without having to depend on anyone else. That's a wonderful feeling I wish I could duplicate in the rest of my life."

*Relying more on one's own resources.* Working out alone teaches independence and self-reliance. "It's not easy to get out of bed every morning at six-ten to hit the road. The challenge is not only in completing the run, but in beginning it, to keep the commitment to myself. Who will know, or who will care, if I turn over and go back to sleep? I get so much more out of my solo runs because I have to invest more energy to get them done. I have to push myself to run further and faster because there is nobody else there to do it for me. I notice over the years this self-reliance has been extended to other areas of my life."

*Improving self-discipline.* Those people who work out by themselves are more internally motivated than those who rely on the support of others. It takes a special resolve to make a commitment to keep going when you are the only one who will know you stopped. An aerobics devotee shares her special method for reinforcing self-discipline when working out alone:

"I start the aerobics while I picture my fat cells burning themselves up. I think about something I ate in the past twenty-four hours that I want to burn off, and I try to imagine how many calories I'm really working off. When I do toning exercises, I picture my leg muscles getting sleeker, my stomach flatter, and my arms more muscular. It's all inspiring to keep my interest during a workout and keep me pushing myself to keep going."

*Practicing being alone.* Working out is one way to learn to be in your own company without feeling unduly restless, bored, or anxious. Since there is a specific goal to be accomplished—twenty minutes on the rowing machine, one hundred sit-ups, a three-mile run, or thirty laps in the pool—exercise provides a structure for being alone. This routine represents a commitment to taking care of yourself, not only to reduce your waistline and tone your muscles, but just as importantly, to find regular time to be with yourself.

The practice of Tai Chi is an example of a paradoxical activity that can take place in a large group, yet stimulates an inner focus in which it feels as if the participant is alone. One practitioner of this ancient form of exercise describes the kind of structure that allows him to retreat into himself even in a crowd of other people:

"It is a strange feeling doing Tai Chi with fifty other people. I mean, here I am, surrounded by other people, maybe I have three square feet to myself, and yet I feel completely isolated. Once we start moving together in slow motion a part of me follows and matches the pace of every other person, but a much greater part of me closes off the world and goes deep inside myself. There is so much to concentrate on—whether my back is aligned, the position of my chin, the placement of my feet and hands, the exact space between my fingers, every muscle loose and relaxed, every part of me focused on what I'm doing. There is just no time to consider anything else. In fact, the appeal of doing Tai Chi for me is it is the one thing I can do without doing anything else at the same time."

*Reducing stress and promoting exhilaration.* There are few activities as tranquil yet invigorating as a long walk, run, swim, or bicycle ride by yourself. Vigorous exercise stimulates the nervous system in a way that not only creates a mental "high," but also dissipates stress. If nothing else, you are temporarily distracted from the conflicts and problems of life because of the concentration that is required to keep moving.

"When I exercise I like to be out in the fresh air. I prefer to be alone because I can go for as long as I want to, when I want to, in whatever direction I want to go in. So I take different routes when I go for hikes. I love to wander.

"Last Sunday I went for a walk by myself. I could see clouds were gathering and wondered if I would be able to get back home before it started to rain. I walked for one hour with the overcast sky and then walked back in the rain for another hour. At first, when the drops started to fall, I felt alarmed. I thought: 'Oh, no. I'm going to get sopping wet.' But then I said to myself: 'Why not enjoy it?' As soon as I did, I noticed the droplets on the trees that looked like little crystals. I tasted the rain coming down my face. And the rocks glistened all around me. It was like I was part of everything around me. That's why I exercise alone—that feeling of being part of something bigger than me."

*Improving self-esteem and confidence.* People who take care of their bodies have a better self-image. They feel more vibrant, more alive, more attractive and healthy. And from this improved body image comes greater self-respect and poise.

"Sure the physical part of running is hard. But I don't really consider that anymore. I mean, when I wake up in the morning, I don't ask myself if I'm going to brush my teeth or not this morning; I just do it. It's the same with running. I don't give myself the choice of whether I want to go out in the rain or snow or heat; I just do it. But the hardest thing for me is not the physical strain. That's only pain, no big deal. I struggle with the things I can't avoid inside my head when I run. After about a mile or two I start to feel really relaxed and my mind starts to wander. Inevitably, seemingly of its own accord, it will settle on some area of my life that feels unsettled. I will start thinking about some of my relationships, or confrontations I've been avoiding, or other unfinished business. For a while I tried running with a radio just to drown out my overactive brain, but that seemed to defeat the purpose of why I was running in the first place—that is, to become more comfortable with myself."

Exercise, whether undertaken in the company of others in a dance studio or alone while walking or cycling briskly down an isolated country road, facilitates an inner focus of internal solitude. It encourages you to concentrate completely on what is going on inside of you, including how the different parts of your body are holding up under the strain, as well as what is going on inside your mind. For others, exercise helps them to get out of their heads so that they can turn off the brain. People also report feeling a greater sense of confidence that comes from developing a level of self-discipline most others never achieve. The exerciser endures pain, discomfort, lungs begging for more oxygen and legs aching for some relief—all for the satisfaction that accompanies such a commitment to self.

Exercising alone helps you to feel more at home inside your body and mind. It releases tension and stress that accumulate during social and work-related obligations. It gives you the time to consider issues you find fascinating and problems you find perplexing. And like any meditative process, exercising increases your capacity for self-discipline in other areas of your life.

## MEDITATION

Although a meditative state of mind can, and often does, occur spontaneously, people report the greatest benefits when they engage in such practices on a regular basis. Like journaling, which promotes self-awareness; exercising, which stimulates self-healing; and studying, which facilitates wisdom, meditation is an example of how private moments can be used to strengthen the ability to be both self-directive and self-reflective.

Meditation is any activity that helps you to turn your attention inward to promote greater relaxation and enlightenment. Most forms of meditation bring on heightened awareness of internal feelings and increased vigor and energy, inducing a state of tranquility and transcending ordinary consciousness to a mystical state that allows for deeper levels of appreciation and understanding.

There are literally hundreds of different meditative techniques designed to produce the same desired effects. Practitioners of transcendental meditation repeat a mantra to themselves. Some Buddhist practices involve concentrating on breathing. Eskimos carve circles in the ground with a stone. Yogis stare at an object such as a design or a vase. Sufis spin around in a circular dance. In his investigations on meditation, psychologist Robert Ornstein summarizes the commonalities of all approaches:

> If we review the extraordinary diversity of the techniques of concentrative meditation in different cultures at different times, one general similarity seems to appear: no matter the form or technique, the essence of meditation seems to consist of an attempt to restrict awareness to a single, unchanging source of stimulation for a definite period of time. In many traditions, the successful achievement of this is termed *one-pointedness of mind*.

Most people envision the formal variety practiced by yogis in lotus position or people repeating a mantra with their eyes closed. However, everyone experiences the meditative state at least a few times each day without consciously realizing it. This happens every time you tune out the external world to insulate yourself from physical and psychological noise and listen to the voice within you. As one woman explains, spontaneous revelations can occur during the most ordinary of moments:

"I was standing at the sink washing dishes, just like I do every night of my life. I could barely hear the voices of my family in the background over the sound of the rushing water. I was just standing there, working automatically, scraping, washing, rinsing, when I seemed to leave my body completely—it was as if I was outside of myself watching me continue to function. My attention became completely focused on everything that was happening. I noticed the feel of the suds on my fingers, the bright colors of the discarded food going down the drain, the sound of the water. Before I knew it, twenty minutes had passed. I have no idea when everyone else left the room. The dishes were all clean. And I felt elated, and more relaxed than I have felt in a long time. It was as if this perfectly ordinary activity helped me to go inside myself, to turn off my brain, and simply be with myself and what I was doing."

Naomi Humphrey, an authority on meditative techniques, believes that private moments such as those described above are the key to any spiritual awakening: "Meditation, unlike intellectual thinking, has the power to put us in touch with ourselves. It actively unites our consciousness and creates a sense of personal wholeness which is so often lacking. This sense of completeness becomes a firm foundation which we may build upon."

Meditative states can occur when you stare at a fire, lost in thoughts you can't really remember; or lie on a beach, feeling the sun warm your body; or look out the window of a plane at the clouds and the vastness of the earth; or are moved to prayer or spiritual communion when you feel the need for guidance and comfort. They are altered states of consciousness characterized by (1) focused concentration, (2) suspension of rational thought processes in favor of deliberate nothingness, (3) a shift from an outward to inward orientation, and (4) a state of mysticism or spirituality in which one feels a connection to the larger universe of Nature, God, or other living things.

All these characteristics play important parts in the meditative activity of Stephen, an attorney who leads a hectic life dictated by court appearances, client consultations, and endless paperwork. Yet through very stressful days in which he must juggle many different tasks, he is renowned among his colleagues and friends for his apparently effortless ability to stay unruffled. He is surprised that others believe his serenity comes naturally to him—for he has studied meditation and practiced faithfully, twice daily, for fifteen years. In a poetic style, he describes the many benefits meditation brings him:

"I suppose I have more mental clarity and less fatigue. When I meditate in the morning it's to set me up for the day, to get my brain waves firing in the right direction, to help me to feel more organized and in control.

"The objective of my afternoon or evening session is more restorative. If I were to take a nap, I would probably feel groggy afterwards. But when I meditate, I always feel wonderful. I feel refreshed and invigorated, as if a whole day's stress and fatigue have vanished. It feels like I'm starting the day over again. I have more patience, more energy, more calmness afterwards. So I do it not so much because I love the meditation experience, but I like what it does for me.

"The experience itself feels like a warm bath. It's like I'm aware of where I am, but I'm not really thinking about it or anything else. I'm just kind of floating, immersed in it. It's all around me. It's very soft. There aren't any jagged edges when I'm in that meditative state."

Practitioners describe meditation as far more than an efficient nap, for it produces an altered state of consciousness that can lead to a deeper self-understanding in addition to its usefulness in recharging energy. It represents one of the most effective ways to turn private moments into the most invigorating, tranquil, and satisfying experiences of daily life.

## ASTRONAUTS OF INNER SPACE

Meditative experiences that produce altered states of consciousness have been intensified through experiments in complete isolation. John Lilly, dubbed the "Astronaut of Inner Space," was credited with inventing the first sensory deprivation tank for studying the effects of solitude on human perception. In this environment, Lilly and his subjects lay in buoyant water heated to precisely 93 degrees Fahrenheit—a temperature at which the body feels neither hot nor cold. The box was perfectly soundproofed and darkened, blocking out all external distractions. By immersing himself in this thoroughly neutral setting, Lilly was better able to experience "inner space" in much the same way that the Morita therapist mentioned in an earlier chapter seeks to help people confront their solitary existence.

After tinkering with variables to make his isolation chamber completely devoid of stimulation, Lilly was astonished to discover the results. He found that after prolonged exposure (at least an hour or two) to total isolation, normal people would begin to reach altered states of consciousness, sometimes to the point of auditory and visual hallucinations. Just as surprising, schizophrenic people would hallucinate *less* often and less intensely than they had outside the tank. Apparently, once freed from the impact of external stimulation, the solitary brain reacts to residual images and begins spontaneous firing of the nervous system. If you close your eyes for a few minutes and still try to "see" what is in the darkness, you will get a taste of what happens in sensory isolation.

Those who practiced in their isolation tanks eventually learned to filter out the internal "noise" from their minds. They found they were able to reach states of tranquility they never knew were possible. After several hours in total solitude they could suspend themselves in calmness and emerge from the tank refreshed and invigorated. They seemed to be able to multiply the effects of meditation to the point where life-changing insights sometimes resulted.

Beth is one such astronaut of inner space. Several times each month, depending on her work schedule and family obligations, she plans a "float" in an isolation tank:

"The first time it was very frightening. Here I was about to go on a journey in which all my senses would be cut off. Wherever I went inside my mind, what if I didn't come back? I took off all my clothes. I put in earplugs. And I climbed inside this coffinlike thing. When the door closed, I started to panic. I couldn't see or hear or feel a thing. I felt so utterly alone. I tried to reassure myself, again and again, that it was safe. After a while I forgot to tell myself these messages. I stopped caring where the door was and stopped trying to calculate how long I had been in there. I just totally relaxed. I surrendered into it. I felt so spacious. And then I remembered I wasn't telling myself where the door was!

"I jerked back to being afraid again. But then I heard this voice inside my head telling me that nothing happened, everything was fine. I could get out whenever I wanted. It has taken me a long time to feel comfortable in there, to be able to surrender to the experience and let go. Since that time I have been back in the tank over a hundred times, and finally I can fully relax. But floating, for me, is something much more than relaxation. I know this will sound strange, but it is practice for death.

"Death is the ultimate in an alone experience. I'm not so

afraid of the pain of dying, or even what will happen afterwards; I'm afraid of going there alone. If I practice being
completely alone, it feels to me like it won't be so hard to
die when the time comes."

Beth's revelations are not unique, as spiritual and religious pilgrims have isolated themselves since the beginning
of recorded history. Jesus, Confucius, Moses, Mohammed,
and Buddha all began solitary quests of contemplation and
enlightenment that are now emulated in monasteries around
the world. From such spiritual retreats into inner space it is
possible to gain a greater closeness to one's inner core as
well as to a higher power.

## SOLITARY PRAYER

In one sense, meditation is a ritualized form of prayer that
is directed inward rather than outward; in both activities
the object is often to lose oneself in the process of connecting with a higher power. For this reason meditation has
existed for thousands of years among ancient religions such
as Buddhism, Hinduism, Judaism, and Islam. More recent
religions, such as Christianity, have based many prayers on
the mystical heritage of meditative practices. In addition to
the benefits, those who pray report a number of other mystical and growthful gains, including feeling more optimism
and hope for the future, feeling there is a purpose and
meaning to daily life, and sometimes experiencing a sense
of exaltation and ecstasy.

A woman describes how prayer helps her feel more calm
and peaceful during her long daily commutes:

"I remember always praying to God ever since I was a
little girl. My mother would always recite prayers to us at
dinner each night. And we all learned to memorize them.
But to me, that's not really praying, at least not in a personally meaningful way.

"I haven't gone to church in years. Actually, the only time I pray is when I'm in my car. I pray out loud when I'm driving around; I talk to God, or at least my image of who God is. I talk through problems I'm having and ask for guidance and support. Of course, I never get any direct answers. But when I'm talking to God driving around in the privacy of my car, I always feel better afterwards. I feel really cared for. I feel understood.

"When I drive home from work each night, it takes thirty or forty minutes. Instead of listening to the radio, I listen to myself talk to God. I tell him what is going on inside me. I ask for his help in being more honest with myself and others. Usually, when I try to tell people what is going on with me, they don't really listen to me; they just give me advice or tell me what to do. But when I pray, I'm able to tell my story without being interrupted or misunderstood. God doesn't tell me what to do, and I appreciate that. I believe I'm perfectly capable of figuring things out myself."

While the car may be an unusual place for someone to offer solitary prayer, any place where privacy or mental retreat is possible will do. Whether kneeling by the bed, sitting in a quiet church or on a hilltop, even cruising down the highway, spiritual and religious activities are often practiced during private moments. What is interesting is how rarely people confide to one another about *how* they pray, as if to do so would break the confidentiality between themselves and God. Others, such as this recovering alcoholic, avoid speaking of their spiritual activities because they feel so self-conscious:

"When I pray, I feel stupid—like I'm not doing it right— like I'm not connecting the way other people do. I try real hard to connect with God and often I feel like no one is there. But sometimes I feel a little chill and a surge of power and then I just know I'm not alone. When I jog, or walk, or when I'm driving by myself, I try to talk to God; it motivates me throughout the day. And I start each morning praying to remind myself that I need a power greater than myself to help me through the day."

In their study of spiritual enlightenment, researchers John Cohen and John Phipps found that those who actively pray are likely to feel less tension and more hope in their lives than those who do not pray. They also feel a greater sense of control over their lives and feel more optimistic about the future. Another religious scholar, William Hulme, prescribes a close relationship to God as a way to reach spiritual enlightenment:

> Communion with God takes place through prayer. The usual image we have of praying is a person with the head bowed, perhaps on bended knees, expressing needs and concerns to God in silence. Actually prayer is more a way of life than a distinct activity, even as friendship is more the awareness in memory or in reality of a comfortable presence than of specific conversations.

Hulme, and others who feel a strong connection to a Being greater than themselves, describe a tremendous comfort available during times of difficulty. It is not only reassuring to have a loving, accepting God as a constant companion, it is also a means for rekindling faith, hope, inner peace, and spiritual enlightenment. Many people experience their relationship with God as an antidote for the anguish of alienation and aloneness. There is always someone who cares, who will listen without judging. This strong and unswayable belief in God, who cannot be touched directly or seen, leaves one to trust intuitive faith. And if one can believe in a Supreme Being that exists only in one's mind and heart but not in the physical world, then one can further trust one's own inner resources to crawl out of solitary discontent.

People thus turn to prayer for strength during times of isolated crisis—surviving a divorce or death of a loved one, rebounding from disappointment, recovering from illness.

Others communicate with God on a more regular and ritualized basis for support, exercising the same degree of self-
discipline and commitment that meditation and other self-
directed activities require.


## CONFRONTING RESISTANCE

Many of the self-directed activities and self-nurturing behaviors covered in this and the previous chapter are those
in which you voluntarily separate yourself from others.
When you are working on a project, exercising, meditating,
or studying, family members and friends may feel neglected
because of your focus on personal needs. In relatively benign form, others may pressure you to relinquish your private moments through complaints and nagging: "What are
you doing *that* for? Why can't you spend more time with
me? Do you *have* to work on that again?" Assuming that
you do spend quality time with the people you love and are
not narcissistically obsessed with your own selfish interests
to the exclusion of others, those most likely to resist your
commitment to solitude are those who have difficulty understanding the attractions of time alone because of their
own unresolved issues.

More vigorous resistance will arise from those who feel
threatened by your need for privacy, as if they fear that
temporary isolation may lead you to leave them behind.
There is some merit to this fear—when one person in a
relationship is working hard on himself or herself and the
other remains stagnant, there *is* a danger that the distance
between them will increase. In spite of how others offer
their support, often they prefer you the way you are. Change
in any aspect of your being means that they will have to
accommodate or grow themselves—and that's a burden
some people don't relish.

Whenever people make any significant changes in their lives they encounter resistance—not just in others who liked things fine the way they were, but also in themselves. Let's say you decide to start modestly by spending part of each week in your own company devoted to some solitary activity you have never tried before—meditation, journal writing, visiting museums, whatever. Even such an innocent alteration in life routines might be misunderstood by family and friends. ("Wait a minute, let me get this straight—you are not joining us because you'd prefer to be all by yourself?")

Negotiation and compromise seem to be the key to following through with solitary activities that are important to you while enlisting the support of others. It takes time to train others to be more tolerant of your independent actions, to help them feel reassured that your solitude does not isolate you from them. People may need to be educated that your private moments allow you to recharge your energy so that you can give even more love. However, by modeling the commitment you have to taking care of yourself and accomplishing the things that are important to you, you can become an inspiration for others.

Self-directed and self-reflective activities are usually undertaken to help you feel better about yourself. This inner peace allows you to function more effectively in your work, family, friendships, and community. You may encounter resistance from others, and occasionally inconvenience, discomfort, or unpredictable responses in yourself. Yet when you feel productive and fulfilled in how you use your opportunities for solitude, the effort is well worthwhile.

# 7

# *Being Spontaneous and Playful*

$S$OLITUDE NEED NOT be "serious" to be satisfying or even productive. In fact, some of the most memorable
times can be playful or even silly. Nowhere is this more
evident than those times when, utterly alone and unobserved, you act completely spontaneous and free. You talk
to yourself with abandon. You act goofy or childlike. You
play games of make-believe. And you give maximum vent to
your spontaneous desires.

Acting out playful urges often falls within the province of
dawdling; however, such periods of unstructured solitude
also serve as a balance for those times requiring a high
degree of self-discipline and sustained work. They help rest,
relax, and divert your mind so that you can resume productive activities with a fresh perspective and renewed energy.

For example, one harried college professor is frequently
tied up with meetings, classes, research projects, and demands from colleagues and students. Every aspect of his life
is so structured and scheduled that he rarely has time to
himself. Imagine, then, the joy he felt upon unexpectedly
discovering an unscheduled afternoon to himself:

"At first it took me a while to adapt to this novelty of
time on my hands with nothing I absolutely had to do. Oh,
there are always things I *could* do—reading papers and
such—but for all practical purposes I was accountable to no
one else for a solid block of time. I sat on the patio and felt
a sense of panic. My gosh, this is such a gift! What should I
do with this time?

"As I began to relax and slow down the pace of my brain, I kicked off my shoes, then my socks. It felt good to feel my toes wiggling without constraint, so I said 'Screw it!' and I took off *all* of my clothes. Have you ever noticed that you don't have to worry how you look when it's just yourself to impress?

"I just sat there and soaked up the sun. I thought of all the things I wanted to do—write a letter, read a magazine, the usual stuff. But then I thought it might be fun to be more spontaneous. Since I was already buck naked I was feeling a bit wicked. There are some things I had always wanted to do but felt too inhibited. First, I turned on a soap opera—I had never seen one before, except on the way to turning the channel to some other show. It was great fun! Next I went upstairs and began pacing, thinking about other things I had always wanted to try. I went into my wife's dresser and took out some of her slinky things to try on. I put on her underwear and lingerie and then modeled them in front of the mirror. I felt goofy as hell, and I was also a bit embarrassed by my behavior. I have this reputation for being so proper. If people could only have seen me then!

"Seeing myself in the mirror wearing a peach-colored teddy sobered me up a bit, so I changed into a sweat suit, eager to move on to something else. I was like a kid in a candy store, afraid this would be my last chance to ever sample these delights again. When I was hungry I ate dessert *first*, then I tried some strange combinations of food. Finally, I worked my way into the study and I played some of my favorite pieces of music, directing the musicians with a flourish. Needless to say, I was very disappointed when the afternoon ended. By the time my wife arrived home, she found me, as usual, reclining in the library, a Bach sonata playing softly, and a stack of student papers on my lap."

This professor's spontaneous afternoon illustrates the ways life can be enriched by letting yourself become more playful when you are alone. You can teach yourself to be more free, more uninhibited, and more self-accepting, thus able to follow your own inner voice without concern for how you may appear to others.

## TALKING TO YOURSELF

One common form of spontaneous solitary play is talking to oneself—grunts and exclamations, long involved conversations, whispered words of encouragement or self-criticism. Although private self-talk may involve little more than giving yourself advice as if you were a wise friend, there is an undeniable element of play involved. When you talk to yourself you are taking on certain roles, trying on different points of view to hear how they sound.

An ultrarespectable attorney confessed a penchant, which his friends and family would never suspect, for speaking to himself in strange voices:

"I've always been rather melodramatic. Before I studied law, I had hoped for a career in drama. The courtroom is simply a stage that is much more lucrative to perform in. For as long as I can remember, I used to talk to myself. My parents got a kick out of it—I think they thought it was more cute than weird. So I felt encouraged and not all that self-conscious about my little games. When I'm driving, going for a walk, or alone in my office or home, I carry on conversations with myself in different voices. There's one voice that sounds sort of silly. There's a know-it-all voice that's kind of a baritone. I've got about a half dozen different ones that I use on a regular basis."

Most monologues occur when people are alone—in the car, during a walk, or around the house—lest other people think them crazy. Indeed, people who talk to themselves indiscriminately may end up in mental hospitals. Of course, the difference between sanity and insanity is not only a

matter of the frequency and intensity with which you talk to
yourself, but whether you are caught doing it.

Speaking thoughts aloud conveys messages on different
levels, since you are not only thinking an idea but also saying it and hearing it. Thus, people talk to themselves when
they're alone to think more clearly, to test the sound of a
plan, as well as to keep themselves company. A librarian
who spends quite a bit of time reshelving books talks to
herself to avoid boredom and to solve perplexing problems:

"One of the things I do a lot is talk to myself. I don't
mean just an occasional mumbled profanity under my
breath; I mean I really carry on lengthy animated conversations. Especially if I'm trying to make an important decision, I will talk out loud listing all the advantages and dis-
advantages. Sometimes I will even sort of act out different
positions, just check out what it would feel like to act a
certain way. Most of the time, though, I just keep up a
running patter—reflecting on what I'm doing or wish I was
doing instead."

Many people I interviewed reported that talking to themselves brought a degree of comfort as well as entertainment.
A woman I spoke with has always found it difficult to be
playful, especially around other people. At parties, meetings, or any social gathering, she fades into the background,
unable and unwilling to be herself for fear of being disapproved of by others. But it is a completely different story
when she is alone:

"I grew up on a farm. When I was a kid I used to take
bike rides, *long* bike rides. I used to do plays while I would
ride. I would do a whole cast of characters. It never seemed
like *I* was ever there; rather, the characters would talk to
one another through me. I was just the audience who would
watch the drama unfold before me.

"Now that I've outgrown my bike, I still play out these
dramas while I drive around in my car. I have this voice that

BEING SPONTANEOUS AND PLAYFUL                                147

nobody else has ever heard. It sounds very theatrical, sort of
like a British actor or politician. It's the same voice I've been
using since I was nine years old. I never plan this. The voice
sometimes just comes out of me when I'm alone, advising
me, supporting me, questioning me. The thing is, I always
feel better after doing one of these dialogues or plays."

An older woman who lost her husband several years ago
also finds much relief from her solitary monologues. When
she is alone, especially in the car where she is certain not to
be overheard, she talks to him as if he were still alive:

"I just feel so lonely sometimes. I miss him so much.
Somehow, I just got in the habit when I'm by myself to talk
to him just as I always did. The only difference is that he
used to drive; now I do. I know I must look like a crazy old
lady talking away as I do, but when you've reached my age, I
think you're entitled to do as you like."

Talking to yourself thus supplies a degree of companionship and comfort during times when you are in the mood
for company, even if it is just another part of yourself acting
the part. This is especially true when the way you speak
to yourself is largely supportive ("Keep going. You're doing fine. Just a little more. Good job!") rather than self-
denigrating ("Damn it. I can't do this! I'm such an idiot!").

## ACTING OUT FANTASIES

Another type of playful activity people enjoy in solitude is
acting out fantasies of their secret selves. People who are
relatively uninhibited are able to vent these spontaneous
urges and thus get in touch with a part of themselves that
has remained basically intact since childhood. Perhaps the
most common example is when you find yourself singing
along while listening to music, or "conducting" a symphony
playing on your stereo. Other people play an "air guitar"

and imagine themselves as the world's greatest rock star, or use their finger to shoot characters on the TV screen, or strike bodybuilder or ballerina poses in front of the mirror.

A man in his late thirties describes how uninhibited and playful he becomes when he is alone, sometimes acting out fantasies reminiscent of his childhood:

"Our house is littered with the wreckage and implements of destruction common to the arsenal of most little boys. My son has the usual assortment of Thundercat swords, Masters of the Universe weapons, G.I. Joe devices, Uzi squirt guns, Laser Tag pistols, and battery-operated stun guns. There are times when I'm alone in the house and I will pick up one of my son's toys. My favorite is the Uzi squirt gun that shoots thirty feet. I pretend I am under attack by enemies of unimagined ruthlessness—some days it might be aliens, other times Ninjas or Commandos. I move carefully throughout the house, dodging traps and ambushes, diving into couches, plotting counterattacks, staging battle scenes. If I'm really in the mood, and the house is particularly thick with infidels, I pull out all the stops and start lobbing hand grenades into dark corners (rolled-up socks make great grenades). Usually I never have more than fifteen minutes to play before I have to get to work, but it brings back such fun memories being a kid in my own world."

A college student shares another example of the kinds of fantasies that are often acted out in solitude:

"I like to shoot baskets in my driveway. I can do it for hours—practicing different shots, pretending I'm playing the Lakers. There's one game I like to play with myself. I pretend that some girl I'm really interested in will approach me if I can make seven out of ten shots. Then I imagine all the things she'll do to me if I make a skyhook shot or sink three free throws in a row. Sometimes I just use the basket like Tarot cards or a Ouija board in that I ask an important question and let the ball determine what the answer will be."

When acted out, solitary fantasies become more real. This is not only satisfying for its entertainment value, but helpful in working out problems under conditions that approximate reality. One woman enjoys rehearsing confrontations of things she wished she had said to people who intimidate her:

"I imagine myself absolutely humiliating my boss in front of the whole office. We have this chair at home that looks a bit like the one my boss has—at least it's big and reminds me of him. I picture him sitting there so smugly and I scream at him and tell him what a selfish, insensitive jerk he really is. It is *so* satisfying!"

Acting out your frustrations and resentments in this way is cathartic. When you keep such feelings to yourself, neither expressing them directly nor releasing them when you are alone, anger often builds inside. These feelings can be dissipated during times when you give yourself permission to regress to a childlike level of play—talking to make-believe characters, pretending you are directing a philharmonic orchestra, trying on wigs or crazy clothing, speaking in strange accents, or engaging in any one of a number of other activities that could be viewed as forbidden or rebellious.

## FORBIDDEN FRUITS.

There is a tremendous thrill in doing things when you are alone that others might disapprove of. After all, you usually bristle a bit at being told you can't do something, even if you don't especially want to do it anyway. As a teenager you wanted to do many things that your parents specifically forbade. They may have told you to stay away from a certain friend, or not to see a movie they felt was in bad taste, or to avoid a certain place. They warned you as well to stay away from things like drinking, eating junk food, smoking, and experimenting with drugs, as well as personal habits such as masturbation and nail biting.

Yet you did some of these things anyway. It was your way of showing you couldn't be controlled completely, that you had a mind of your own and could make your own decisions. You discovered that not only were your parents sometimes wrong in their pronouncements, it was even more exciting to do prohibited things behind their backs.

Most of us use solitude to act out our rebellious urges, getting a special kick out of doing something that feels forbidden. Many people I interviewed reported occasionally doing things that nobody has ever discovered. One of the most common examples is described by a teenager who feels a special thrill engaging in forbidden practices in the kitchen:

"One of the best things about being alone in the house is whenever I'm thirsty I can just drink milk or Coke directly from the bottle. I also like to reach into the different bowls where my mom keeps leftovers and taste different stuff with my fingers. She'd kill me if she knew."

Most people tend to operate under different rules of etiquette when they're eating alone. This is true not only for what you eat and how much you eat, but also how you eat it. A simple example of this point occurs when you drop food on the floor—not just any food, but the last piece of cheese, fruit, or cake in the refrigerator. You would, of course, throw it out if there were other people around; it looks unseemly to just rinse it off and pop it in your mouth. But would you necessarily do so when you are alone?

There are prescribed taboos surrounding food preparation and consumption in every culture: for example, the prohibition against eating certain animals (pigs in the Middle East, cows in India, pigs and shellfish among religious Jews, cats in North America), and the ways in which food is eaten (such as not eating with the left hand in certain cultures, or chewing with the mouth closed in our own society).

In writing about the origins of these cultural taboos, anthropologist Marvin Harris explains how certain animals became the object of religious sanctions because they were too expensive to raise, or because their continued use might endanger the existing mode of subsistence. That is why, for example, we don't eat cats (which are needed to keep the rat population down), or eat from communal plates (through which disease might spread). But once we are beyond others' scrutiny, normal rules of food consumption are temporarily suspended.

Whether in the dead of night or during daylight hours when others in the house are otherwise occupied, solitary eating is often quite a different experience from dining out at a restaurant or at a social gathering. In my research into what people do in the kitchen when nobody else is around, the following behaviors emerged as the most common:

*Sneaking foods that are not part of a prescribed diet.* So much of what we do in life is for the benefit of others' approval. In the case of sneaking forbidden foods, we don't want our doctor or family to know that we are not sticking with a diet that is in our best interests. It is almost as if we believe that if nobody sees us go off the diet, it doesn't really count. This is the same magical reasoning that allows us to believe such notions as that the calories from a diet soda will cancel those of a candy bar; the crumbs of cookies lose their calories in the process of being broken up; foods consumed for "medicinal" purposes are good for us (brandy, hot chocolate, prune Danish).

It is funny how we attempt to justify these inconsistencies. A woman who is usually quite diligent about following a diet low in fats and cholesterol confessed that she occasionally sneaks into the kitchen if she thinks nobody will see her:

"Periodically, according to some cycle I don't understand completely, I feel this urge to binge on ice cream. Maybe it's related to stress or something and I need to just indulge myself without limits. I notice I will plan the deed days in advance. Rarely have I ever impulsively gone out to do it. I keep an extra half gallon of chocolate fudge ripple in the freezer. I wait until the house is quiet and I know I won't be interrupted. Then I sit down right by the freezer so if I hear somebody coming I can slip it back in. And then I eat the whole thing. I mean if I'm going to eat, I might as well *really* eat."

Sneaking foods we are not supposed to have begins early in life, as my seven-year-old disclosed after I promised I would never tell his mother: "When my mom goes out and leaves me with the cleaning lady, I pig out on food. I climb up onto the counter and I reach into the cupboard to get cookies. So far nobody has ever noticed."

*Eating with your fingers.* In a number of societies, eating with the hands is considered perfectly acceptable. Our Western culture has evolved the use of eating utensils, which we consider to be more efficient and sterile. However, tremendous pleasure can be derived from eating with the fingers, and sometimes it is more convenient when you are standing in front of an open refrigerator and just want a nibble. One man waxes especially poetic about the joys of eating with his hands:

"If I could have my way, I would do it all the time. There's an African restaurant I go to a lot because I can actually eat with my fingers in public. Usually, I have to do it on the sly. I think my wife knows about my little secret, but she has never said anything to me about it. Another thing I do is take things off other people's plates when they're not looking—at least if I don't think I can be caught. The other night I was out with a friend and he ordered shrimp, which I love. When he went to make a phone call I reached over and grabbed one. He sat down, looked at his plate as if he thought one was missing, but then shrugged it off. I supposed I could just ask people if I could have a little taste, but that wouldn't be near as much fun."

*Making unusual food concoctions.* When you are alone you are also more likely to experiment with food combinations that others might consider strange or disgusting. One man who likes to be inventive in the kitchen when nobody else is around describes some of his creative ideas:

"I love to experiment making different kinds of sandwiches. Since my family tends to be repulsed by my various masterpieces, this is an activity I tend to do when I'm alone. I might try chopped liver, sardines, Bermuda onions, and dill pickles on rye, with a splash of thick mustard. Or I'll just put something together with whatever happens to be in the refrigerator—maybe a leftover pancake stuck into pita bread with pea pods, red peppers, and vanilla yogurt. Hey, what's the difference? It all ends up in the same place anyway."

Many of the things you do when you are alone involve catering to your most personal tastes—eating exactly what you feel like, just the way you want it, without compromising for anybody. You can skip dinner completely and eat only dessert. You can wipe your hands on your lap or wipe your face on your sleeve. You can belch without having to excuse yourself. You can drink out of the bottle and eat with your fingers. Or you can feel free to use impeccable manners just as you would at a formal occasion.

## SECRET SELVES

Not everyone outgrows the natural curiosity of the child or the rebelliousness of the teenager. As we have seen, many people live in a secret world when they are by themselves— living out fantasies, pleasuring themselves in private, sneaking around to do things they would never do in front of others. These secrets can run the gamut from the most

innocent act of writing in a private diary or sneaking a cig-
arette on the porch, to voyeuristic acts of observing other
people's private worlds.

In chapter 9 we will deal with the more insidious forms
of private behavior, but there are also a number of relatively
benign manifestations of the secret self. We could all agree
that some private behaviors are self-destructive or indicate
an unhealthy lack of self-control: the alcoholic who sneaks
drinks behind others' backs, for example, or the voyeur
who invades other people's privacy, or the bulimic who en-
gages in binging episodes. However, there are many gray
areas in which the secret self merely acts out that person's
idea of a good time. When such behavior does not violate
other people's rights, represent self-destructive motives, or
result in negative consequences, these private acts can be
harmless when not taken to extremes.

*Recreational drugs.*   If you feel that certain acts will
not be accepted by others, but you feel compelled to do
them anyway, your behavior will be forced underground.
And sometimes it is just downright fun to engage in certain
activities without other people knowing. Sometimes this is
the case with the use of drugs and alcohol to release inhibitions and facilitate playfulness. One man, for example, occasionally likes to smoke marijuana on the sly. He smokes
secretly, he explains, not because his wife would disapprove, but because he enjoys a special thrill of rebellion in
the attempt to do it without her awareness:

"When everyone is upstairs watching TV I sneak into the
basement to smoke a joint. This takes careful planning to
get away with it, although it's just a game. My wife doesn't
care if I smoke, but I get a kick out of trying to fool her. I
never do deceive her since she always smells it on my
breath, but at least she has the decency to act like she
doesn't notice. I don't think I do this that much to get
high—especially since it doesn't even feel that good any-

more. No, I do it mostly for the fun of sneaking. I tiptoe down the steps trying to memorize where the creaks are. I even wear my Indian moccasins to minimize noise. It just feels good to get away from everyone and everything else, if just for a few minutes. Then, when I rejoin my family up-stairs, I stay in my own world for a while. I don't do it to escape reality as much as to intensify my appreciation of it. It becomes a way I can separate myself from the world, go deeper inside to increase my awareness and heighten my perception. I also get a kick out of doing something that nobody else knows I am doing. It kind of reminds me of that special thrill of stealing a cookie without my mother noticing the cookie jar was moved."

The thrill this man experiences in sneaking around is not the only allure of his drug-taking behavior. Mind-altering chemicals induce experiences that can be euphoric, expan-sive, and entertaining, but they can also be frightening and addictive. Except for societies in which drugs are integrated into religious ceremonies, drug use is among the most pri-vate of all experiences. Because certain drugs are outlawed in our society (except for alcohol), and because the effects often produce feelings of withdrawal and introspection, most people prefer to take them in isolation. One of the most common reasons why people experiment with these potentially dangerous and habit-forming substances is their power in reducing inhibitions. When we add to the picture the forbidden aspect of using these chemicals, we can see the incredible allure of sampling them.

*Violating the privacy of others.* Just as with forbid-den acts of sneaking food or drugs, many other solitary behaviors feel thrilling because of their secrecy. Many peo-ple reluctantly admit that when they are alone, even for a few minutes, different rules of conduct and morality govern their behavior. Insatiable curiosity impels people to violate the boundaries of others' privacy. A typical case in point

was supplied by woman who spoke frankly of her clan-
destine activities whenever she finds herself having to wait
at an acquaintance's home:

"Whenever I'm alone for a while in a room, I go through
people's things. I just sort of look through things that are lying
around. If there's enough time for me to be thorough I will
open drawers and closets, look under furniture. I guess I'm
kind of nosy. But I've found some awfully strange things
that people keep right out where you could find them. I
can't believe how trusting some people are. Boy, I'd never
leave anyone alone in my house."

Another example of skulking around in other people's
privacy is illustrated by a young man whose motive for
his reconnaissance missions through people's possessions is
much more than curiosity:

"I've never been very popular with girls. In fact, I haven't
had much experience with them at all. I've seen pictures
and all of naked girls, but I haven't seen one in person.
Many years ago, when I was visiting someone's house—
maybe a relative or a friend of my parents—I started sneaking into the bedroom of the girl, if any female lived in the
house. Everyone else would be eating or talking downstairs
and I would pretend to go to the bathroom, or just slip
away. Then, after I found the right bedroom, I'd look
through the drawers until I found the underwear drawer
and I'd steal a bra. I've been collecting bras for a long time
and I have lots of them. I like to smell them and imagine
that the girl is in the room with me. It's kind of fun to look
at them all, and with each one, to try to picture what the
girl would look like. It's also pretty exciting to add new ones
to my collection. I've never been caught yet."

Another way in which people exhibit their very human
nosiness goes beyond inspecting people's things. There has
always been a sort of voyeuristic allure to the movies, an
illusion that the viewer is spying on the people on screen. A
few individuals carry their voyeuristic urges out of the

theater by looking through the windows of real, live people. These are not officially diagnosed Peeping Toms, but people who occasionally feel the need to satisfy curiosity about what other folks are doing. One gentleman with an unusually high level of curiosity has devised a system for clandestinely observing his neighbors that is only possible in today's urban life:

"I live in an apartment building, one of those tall glass structures. Since my place is on the twenty-ninth floor, I have an unobstructed view of the other buildings around me. I can look out my window and see thousands of other lights winking on and off from the apartment houses all around me. There is one building directly across from me that has about three hundred or four hundred windows I can see into from different angles. In some apartments I can see only chandeliers. In others I can see only people's feet. But in perhaps three dozen windows I can see right into people's lives. I can watch them cooking or watching TV or arguing or doing whatever people do. Naturally, most people close their drapes if they're up to something really good, but you'd be amazed at how many people seem to forget. Or maybe they do it deliberately, or don't care one way or the other.

"I have this telescope that was a present from my uncle when I was a kid. There's no better way to spend an evening alone then to turn off all the lights in my place, roll a joint or open a bottle of wine, and settle in for some entertainment that's better than the movies."

These disclosures typify the kinds of "underground" private moments that can only exist when people are left unmonitored. Societal laws and moral rules are sometimes suspended when people are alone, leading them to engage in activities they would never do with others' knowledge. This is why, throughout the ages, privacy has not been tolerated very well: because of fears that privacy would allow deviant or dangerous behavior to flourish.

## TRANSCENDING CONVENTIONALITY

In spite of the moral transgressions and deviant acts that can occur during private moments, it is precisely because there is a temporary suspension of external monitoring that we are able to feel more free. Because we are more uninhibited, spontaneous, and playful when we are alone, we can transcend conventional limits of conduct and thinking. From such freedom and independence, the most satisfying pleasures are possible—regressing to childhood games, acting ridiculous, enjoying an existence that has few rules or limits except those that *we* impose. It is during such times of privacy and solitude that great creative ideas are born.

# 8

# *Appreciating Fantasy and Creativity*

*E*VERY SECOND OF YOUR life, whether you are awake or asleep, whether you are thinking furiously or are mentally blank, billions of electrical impulses spark through your brain, creating a constant stream of feelings, images, ideas, and sensations. Whenever your brain isn't otherwise occupied, it will naturally drift on its own—from the further reaches of your past to what you might like to experience in the future, from a wildly impractical idea to one that leads you to create something wonderful. This unique private experience continues whether you are alone or in the midst of a crowd.

Apart from this rather random flow of ideas and images, periods of reflection or creation are scheduled into your life on a regular basis. These retreats into fantasy and imagination are more than a way to occupy idle time; they are the basis for developing your personal identity and making sense of the world.

People who enjoy their time alone relish opportunities to consider the meaning of their lives and where they are headed. They question their intentions and actions. They review events from the distant and recent past in order to make plans for the future. They use fantasy as a way to give vent to their creative spirit. Quite simply, they are thinking beings who enjoy the intrinsic pleasures of using their imaginations.

## THE FANTASY LIFE OF OUR
## SECRET SELVES

Creativity involves intense mental activity—the ability to imagine "what ifs," to visualize new variations of things you have seen before. Creativity is sparked by an active imagination and a vivid mental life. The fantasies that fuel imaginative acts are also intrinsically enjoyable as a form of self-entertainment and self-realization. An advertising writer describes a secret self that few people will ever know:

"I am a poet. I have always been a poet and I always will be. Nobody else knows this. The people at work think my whole life's ambition is to keep writing radio spots or cute slogans for new products. But I live to be a poet. I am always thinking about the time I can leave this garbage behind to do serious writing. In the meantime, I occupy myself during lunch hours, coffee breaks, late nights, by being the best poet I can. The thing is, I haven't shown anyone my poems nor submitted any for publication. I know you'd say I'm afraid of rejection, and you'd be right. My fantasies are so perfect of how licentious young ladies will swoon at one of my readings, why take the chance I'll spoil it?"

Retreats into fantasy provide instant solitude during boredom, restlessness, or tension. Whenever you feel the need to divert or to entertain yourself, fantasy provides a ready alternative. When taken in moderate and timely doses, fantasy is much more than an escape from reality; it is an outlet for creative energy. One writer described a protracted inner fantasy he had had earlier that day while standing in line with dozens of fellow workers:

"Some of my best ideas have come during the most public of occasions. I might be at a party, or in the midst of some meaningless conversation I've heard a dozen times before, and I just check out for a minute or two. I'm sure I look pretty much the same to others—I smile and nod my head and such. But I go on these trips inside my head, projecting myself to faraway places, playing mind games, wondering how things would be if only there were certain changes.

"Today I was standing in line at a cafeteria, impatiently and restlessly, when before I knew it, I was wondering what it would be like if I had no expectations in my life. I get disappointed a lot in other people, in lines not moving fast enough, in people letting me down, and I started imagining what my life would be like if I stopped expecting anything from anybody. As hard as that would be for me to do, I was liking how it would feel to never be disappointed again."

Fantasy can include almost any mental activity—imagery, daydreaming, visualization, reveries, ruminations, and streams of consciousness. These occur consciously and unconsciously, spontaneously and in deliberately controlled doses. In all its various manifestations, your fantasy life is the core of your secret self and provides many benefits for your continued mental health.

## VALUES OF FANTASY

Our culture, modeled by our Puritan forefathers, places a premium on hardheaded realism. Most people, therefore, feel some guilt over fantasy activity and worry that it might be harmful. They feel it is the province of artists or the indulgence of dreamers. It is difficult enough to live a life along the straight and narrow path without also having to monitor our private thoughts. We have been taught by parents, teachers, clergy, and the media to feel guilty about "dirty thoughts" or forbidden ideas, as if *thinking* about something that is naughty is the same as actually *doing* it.

Contemporary psychologists such as Jerome Singer have found that fantasies add color and spice to our lives and are a form of creative play that can be further developed to accomplish several purposes:

- A natural analgesic and tranquilizer, fantasy produces feelings of calmness and relaxation. Alpha waves in the brain, heart rate, and blood pressure can all be positively affected by soothing imagery.
- Fantasies help counteract feelings of loneliness. They permit you to conjure up close relationships of the past or loved ones separated by geographical distance.
- Fantasies are clues to your unconscious and thus are a helpful tool for understanding yourself. They provide evidence of your secret unfulfilled desires, repressed wishes, and unresolved conflicts.
- Fantasy is a safe way to explore the world. You can travel anywhere in the universe without spending a dime.
- You can prepare for anticipated struggles and rehearse effective interventions by imagining how things might unfold and how you would react.
- Fantasy is one solution for boredom. No matter how little activity is going on around you, there is always the unlimited potential for entertainment inside your imagination.
- Through fantasy, you can satisfy needs that are beyond your reach because of financial, legal, and moral limitations.
- Exercises in make-believe train both children and adults to enhance their creativity and thinking processes. The power to imagine "What if . . . ?" has led to advances in every scientific and artistic endeavor.

Many of these characteristics are demonstrated in the life of a woman I interviewed who had formerly been a successful sales representative. She attributed much of her excellent job performance to her ability to imagine different outcomes and possibilities in regard to her accounts and to come up with creative solutions. She also fantasized constantly about plotting her rise up the corporate ladder— first as sales manager, then vice president of marketing, finally, as chairwoman of the board. She eventually found her preoccupation with images of power and ambition disturbing, and the texture of her fantasy life began to change:

"Or maybe it's the other way around. Maybe my fantasies changed first, and *that* became the motivator for altering my lifestyle. All I know is that I didn't like myself much anymore spending so much time dreaming about how much money I was going to make and how much territory I would control. Once I got out of that environment I noticed that my fantasies dealt more with wanting to be closer to other people."

Research by Singer and other experts confirms the beneficial effects of fantasy. Children who fantasize a lot exhibit more self-control, better concentration, and less anxiety and frustration. They seem to be better at occupying their time without having to depend on others for diversion. Because they exercise their brains more, they are more flexible thinkers and problem solvers.

As they grow to adulthood, fantasizers cope better with crises and respond better to change than their peers who did not give vent to their imaginations. According to Singer:

The practiced daydreamer has learned the art of pacing so that he can shift rapidly between inner and outer channels without bumping into too many obstacles. He has developed a resource that gives him some control over his future through elaborate planning, some ability to amuse himself during dull train rides or routine work, and some sources of stimulation to change his mood through fanciful inner play.

A well-developed fantasy life, then, would appear to be the foundation for serenity and tranquility. Because fantasy encourages people to be playful, imaginative, and mentally active, fantasizers are also less bored, less prone to drug abuse, and more emotionally healthy than those who stifle their private daydreams.

## WHAT PEOPLE FANTASIZE ABOUT

Several themes seem to crop up again and again in fantasy life. These fantasy areas, while universal in human experience, are also reflective of the individual values held by each of us, whether we long for power, self-control, or excitement. Not unlike our dreams, fantasies say a lot about what is important to us and what we find missing from our lives.

Most fantasies are not exotic in nature but rather involve the most mundane details of daily existence. Proportionately, fantasies about sex are relatively rare (occupying less than 1 percent of our thinking); most common are fantasies that have to do with things like what to fix for dinner, which route to drive home, or the words to a favorite song.

*Sex.*   Sexual fantasies may not be the most common variety of mental imagery, but they are certainly one of the most exciting. On the outside you may appear perfectly calm sitting in a meeting, working at a desk, standing around, even carrying on a casual conversation, when all of a sudden, uninvited but not unwelcome, vivid sexual images dance around your brain. Your heart speeds up, your juices start to flow, and a vague smile crosses your face. This private sensual journey is described by a man who imagines he is the passive recipient of a seduction:

"I'm out doing something, shopping or picking up my laundry, just sort of minding my own business, when this very lost, innocent kind of woman asks for directions somewhere. I attempt to help her out, but she only becomes more and more confused. Finally, I volunteer to show her. But the best part of the fantasy is that I don't really have to do much. I mean, she sort of makes the move and picks *me* up. That's what's so great about it—she seduces *me*. I just go along with her, sort of turn myself over to her plan, whatever she wants."

As this man implies, sexual fantasies can be used quite successfully for diversion and stimulation. They are also helpful as a method of stress reduction, as one woman explains:

"I have a fairly elaborate fantasy ritual I use every night to fall asleep. Sometimes it might take several weeks to get all the way through a particular scenario. It's very erotic. I imagine this perfect guy who can make love twenty-four hours a day, seven days a week, without ever needing time to rest up. It never gets very far because I fall asleep in the middle of it and I have to continue it the following night. It takes at least a few sessions just to set up the plot. The fantasies always have a similar theme, although the location may change. If I don't make up these scenarios, I start to worry about things. So these fantasies really work for me. They help me to relax and focus my attention on something pleasurable before I go to sleep."

*Money.* Typical of money fantasies is one reported by a secretary who makes $17,000 per year and dreams of how added wealth could bring her so much more freedom:

"I think about, more than I would like to admit, what I'd do if I had a steady income of $200,000 a year. I would never have to see my boss again, that arrogant bastard! No more taking orders from anyone ever again. No more depending on anyone else to take care of me. I could get a Porsche, a big house, a brand-new wardrobe. I could travel wherever and whenever I want."

Fantasies of increased wealth are quite common for men and women alike. Money is associated with power, not only over other people, but especially over one's own destiny. People fantasize about limitless wealth because of the freedom, the respect, the power they believe it would give them. In reality, those who are in the upper income brackets derive less satisfaction from wealth than the less fortunate imagine.

A physician who brings in a mid-six-figure salary describes how having money changed the nature of his fantasies, though it failed to give him more freedom:

"The whole time I suffered all the way through medical school I dreamed of having what I have now—but it's ironic, there's no time for me to enjoy it. My accountant put me in these tax shelters that require me to keep my income high in order to reap the benefits. My practice is full and I can't seem to turn away new referrals; my memories are still fresh of what it was like to struggle. Now, in the precious moments of solitude when I'm not in the hospital, my office, or on call, I fantasize about what it would be like have a simpler life."

Nevertheless, many people would love the opportunity to have this man's problems. Perhaps one of the most common dreams today deals with instant riches: for example, one has only to observe the long lines of people waiting to buy lottery tickets. Fifty years ago such dreams centered around the death of a wealthy relative; today they focus on luck bestowing a winning number:

"I pretend I won the lottery and think about all the things I would do with the money. I could quit my job and tell everyone else to take a hike. It's just kind of fun to imagine myself driving around in a limousine, lounging around by the pool, attending society benefits, wearing gorgeous clothes. I don't think about it *all* the time, but once in a while it's kind of fun to think about how things would be different."

*Rehearsing the future.*   Inner activity is often directed toward making plans for the future. Time spent mentally

APPRECIATING FANTASY AND CREATIVITY

structuring various courses of action and predicting what effects they might have allows us to function more productively in the world. Another use for fantasies about the future is to protect ourselves against possible tragedy by anticipating the worst-case scenario and then imagining how we would handle it. A married woman with young children mentally rehearses how she would conduct her life if she should ever lose her husband:

"I imagine how I would go on if my husband died. I don't like to think about this, but I just can't help it. My whole life revolves around him. He has tried to reassure me that I'll be OK, and maybe I would, I don't know. But I still think about how I would live, what I would tell our kids, what decisions I would make, where I would live, just how I would survive."

Fantasies also become a kind of creative dress rehearsal in which we "try on" different lives to see how they might feel. A successful businessman who made a mid-life career switch explains the role his inner fantasy life played in stimulating this change:

"I almost always had this intense desire to help people. The whole time I was dealing in merchandising, marketing, sales, and making a bundle in it, I never really felt much satisfaction. I used to picture myself in various helping professions—as a social worker or policeman in the inner city, as a teacher for the disadvantaged, or a coach for delinquents. All the time I was in therapy, I would imagine myself sitting in my therapist's chair. She seemed so brilliant and together and articulate. And she really got a charge out of helping people—I could tell.

"So there I was sitting in the reception areas of various companies I was doing business with, and I'd be thinking not about their problems, but about the life I wanted to lead. I carried around a notebook in which I would calculate ways I could afford graduate school. I drew plans for a clinic I would run. I designed my ideal office a thousand different ways. I pictured the leather chair I would sit on and the exact configuration of furniture that would hold my clients. I kept a journal of my therapist's best lines, things I would one day use myself."

This inner focus became the impetus for the businessman to fulfill a lifelong dream to make a career change. The fantasy reminded him of the goals that gave his life meaning. By using their imagination, people who feel frustrated and stymied by the constraints of reality can indulge themselves more fully in their private desires.

Fantasies should not be used as a substitute for living but as a supplement to daily life. They are not only a ready antidote for boredom but a stimulator for a more creative, productive life. It is from fantasy that real-life goals are formulated and mastered.

*Reliving the past.*   For the great majority of us, reliving incidents allows us to reexperience highlights of our lives, as well as to avoid repeating our mistakes. In some cases, however, peak experiences that are relived in fantasy become the consolation for a life that has lost some of its luster. An aging beauty queen who was once a finalist in the Miss America pageant reveals:

"I can't tell you how many times I've relived that week in my life. I was on top of the world. I can picture almost every moment, every conversation. I can remember the audience and the judges and the other girls. Nothing since has ever come close. I'm divorced. I'm broke. I have no job. My kids are just about grown. And all I've got are those photos on the wall and my memories."

The mind is a warehouse of stored memories that are kept on file, ready to bring out at a moment's notice. Typical of these reveries is the following disclosure:

"I relive particularly exciting times in my life—those special times I don't want to forget. Things stand out, like a speech I once made to a very enthusiastic audience, when I used to play ball in high school, my first sexual encounter . . . just ordinary stuff that seems important to me."

We also fantasize about what we might have said or done differently if we had the chance to do it all over again. The following woman illustrates this variety:

"Most of what I think about when I'm alone are things I wish I had said to people. Sometimes I get so flustered that I just don't say what I think to people. I let others take advantage of me. My mom is always telling me what to do and how I should live my life. As a matter of fact, everybody seems to put their two cents in. I usually listen to what they have to say, but boy, inside I want to tell them to mind their own damn business! I rehearse these things in my head. I picture myself telling them how I really feel."

*Entertainment.* Fantasies are typically used to pass idle moments during periods of restlessness, boredom, or transitions between other tasks; they may carry little significance other than as a method of self-entertainment. They don't have to be messages from the unconscious, nor do they have to be complex metaphors for unresolved issues in our lives. Sometimes fantasies are just unstructured fun time, opportunities to turn off the censors and let the mind wander where it likes. In moderate doses, fantasy is a pleasant and temporary escape from reality as well as an outlet for creative energy.

One young housewife, who is alone all day in her apartment, entertains herself by imagining the home she would like to have someday: "I think of the ways I would like to build and decorate my dream house. I picture each room, and go through it trying to design the layout and how I would furnish it."

The fantasies are often as varied as the people who have them. The following told by a middle-aged man is typical:

"I pretend I can read people's minds. You know, I sort of guess what they're really like. Especially when I have layover time in an airport, I sit in the waiting area and watch people walk by. I look for patterns. For example, it seems like every time I see someone smoking a pipe, he also seems to be wearing rubbers. I also make up stories about where the people are traveling to and what they'll do when they get there."

Fantasies are indeed clues to our unfulfilled wishes. The themes and content of our daydreams may change over time, as we meet certain needs and develop new goals and interests. Great painters, writers, thinkers, builders, and inventors treat the imagination with utmost respect, for it is the source of inspiration for ideas that can be developed into masterpieces. In all its various forms, fantasy represents that kind of inner solitude that allows us to develop our inner world and creativity.

## SOURCES OF CREATIVE OUTLET

While the act of fantasizing can often be done in the company of others, the realization of fantasy in creativity can only be done alone. Without the insulation from other influences and distractions, it would be difficult to focus your concentration on a uniquely personal vision. It is hard enough to create something new; it is even more difficult when you can't hear your own voice over the roar of others' influences. That is why writer Henry Miller refused to read anything when he was at work on a book: "Every author I fall in love with I want to imitate. If only I could imitate myself."

Although most artists, writers, and thinkers have encountered solitude by choice, a few have had solitude imposed on them. Forced isolation has played a role in fostering the productivity of many writers. A number of the world's most famous authors—Plato, Aristotle, Ovid, Marco Polo, Machiavelli, Martin Luther, Voltaire, Roger Bacon, Daniel Defoe, Victor Hugo, Turgenev, and Dostoyevsky, for example—were imprisoned or banished at one time or another. In most cases the jailers hoped to minimize the writers' "dangerous" ideas. Never did they imagine such deprivation would only make these thinkers more determined, prolific, independent, and creative. Some authors did their best work under these circumstances. Cervantes created Don Quixote while in prison; Sir Walter Raleigh penned his *History of the World* while locked in the Tower of London.

In contemporary society, of course, it isn't necessary to be in prison in order to have the time and space to be creative! Moreover, one needn't be a Plato or a Cervantes to enjoy the thrills and satisfactions of creating something original. However, the most difficult problem in most busy lifestyles is to find enough private opportunities to give vent to creative urges. One psychologist in her forties enjoys creativity in the kitchen:

"My most creative outlet is to get lost in the process of cooking. I have to know that I have an extended period of time to be alone, that all my kids are taken care of, that my husband is otherwise occupied. There can be no interruptions. I can just pace things as I will, which tends to be very slowly. While I'm cooking, or even starting to lay out all the ingredients I will need, my mind starts to wander—I sort of free associate. I find myself jotting down notes of things I have to do. It becomes a time for me to let my mind organize itself by letting it go where it will. It allows me to work through some things in my head at the same time I'm able to achieve something that is important to me—a spectacular torte or delicious soup or crusty soufflé. I feel a level of accomplishment that I don't get to feel very often because the nature of my work is so abstract. I can't walk out of my office at the end of the day and say to myself: 'Look what I did today!' My work is much slower than that and so intangible. So when I'm by myself, I really get into the creative nature of cooking, and being able to look at the result in just a few hours."

This woman feels the constant demands of her children, spouse, friends, and clients. Because her work takes a long time to accrue observable results, she especially values creative tasks that can be completed in a single hour or afternoon. She has also found that other activities, such as quilting, writing poetry, even helping her children with their homework, provide creative outlets for her, but none as satisfying as what she can do in the kitchen.

## WHY PEOPLE CREATE

In his book on solitude, Anthony Storr writes that one of the most pervasive struggles throughout human existence is that between two opposing drives: "the drive for companionship, love, and everything else which brings us close to our fellow men; and the drive toward being independent, separate, and autonomous." According to Storr, it is through the creative process that this paradox may be most healthfully addressed. Creativity requires a degree of isolation and separateness for inspiration to germinate. However, it also requires a person to construct linkages between his or her own visions and the ideas of others. No watercolor, melody, sonnet, invention, or recipe stands alone; it exists within a historical context and forms a bridge between people across time.

Creative acts are offered from the individual to the community as a gift. They appeal, according to Storr, to the human search for order, harmony, unity, and wholeness, while counteracting feelings of alienation and loneliness. Novelist Graham Greene found creative solitude to be the foundation for psychological health and the antidote for despair: "Writing is a form of therapy; sometimes I wonder how all those who do not write, compose or paint can manage to escape the madness, the melancholia, the panic fear which is inherent in the human situation."

Storr writes that such creative people as Rudyard Kipling, Franz Kafka, Ludwig van Beethoven, Emily Dickinson, Alfred Tennyson, and Sylvia Plath are examples of those who converted their sense of depression and helplessness into productive solitary acts. Disappointed in their relationships, they turned their feelings of loss and loneliness into a dynamic form of solitary play. They found solace in the words they wrote and the notes they composed. Unable to feel close to others, they searched throughout their lives to become close to the inner spirit within themselves. They used creative output to structure an order on the outside that they couldn't quite manage on the inside. Storr explains:

> The search for order, for unity, for wholeness is, I believe, a motivating force of single importance in the lives of men and women of every variety of temperament. The hunger of imagination is active in every human being to some degree. But the greater the disharmony within, the sharper the spur to seek harmony, or, if one has the gifts, to *create* harmony.

One need not be a major composer or writer in order to reap the benefits of creative solitude; time spent arranging flowers, building furniture, improvising a recipe, or writing an expressive letter can also allow you to improve the quality of life in your own personal way. People create so that they may stretch themselves, and in the process become more vibrant human beings. Creativity enables you to experience the passion and excitement that accompany the birth of new ideas. It encourages you to feel you are being productive and contributing to the welfare of other people. Finally, creative people report feeling that in some way they have cheated death by leaving some enduring part of themselves behind. As long as some part of you—a story you told or an object you built—remains in the memories of people who knew you, you will, in a sense, continue to exist.

Creativity is, in the words of psychologist Rollo May, a process "representing the highest degree of emotional health, as the expression of normal people in the act of actualizing themselves." People who follow creative pursuits do so not only because they want to but because they often feel they *have* to. It is as if they have no choice but to follow the voice within, which gets louder and louder if it is ignored.

The human drive to be involved in creative activities is illustrated by the experience of an amateur flutist, who begins to feel restless and empty if he doesn't find time alone periodically for several uninterrupted hours of playing:

"It's kind of interesting to me that although I'm in a performance-oriented profession as a training consultant, I have never played the flute in front of an audience. I play for myself and myself only. I don't know if I play well or not. I don't supposed it matters since the music sounds quite beautiful to my own ears.

"So much of my life is repetitive. It's structured by assignments and appointments. Even my low-fat diet is restricted to a few basic food groups. But when I play the flute, whether it is a Handel sonata or my own stuff, I feel completely free. My fingers zip across the silver instrument, incredible sounds coming out that *I* create. . . . It just boggles my mind to think that I can make such beautiful music, that it is *my* mouth and *my* fingers that create the notes. I don't think there is another time in my life I feel more alive except when I am in the throes of an orgasm."

This man really doesn't consider whether he has a choice to play his instrument or not. The consequences of *not* taking time out from his hectic schedule to play are unacceptable—he starts to feel more and more fragmented. The creation of music leaves him feeling refreshed and invigorated, ready to tackle the other problems of his life with greater zeal.

The experience of needing to create to feel alive is shared by a theoretical physicist who has spent the past thirty years constructing models of the ways molecules interact. While his scientific training and technical skills are indeed an important part of his work, the great bulk of his research involves the kind of abstract thinking that requires hours of uninterrupted solitude. In fact, of all the ways he could spend his time, he finds the greatest satisfaction in taking a solid block of time by himself to think about theoretical problems:

"I really *need* to be alone; it's not a preference at all; it's an all-pervasive drive in me that I can't stifle. I must have freedom in my life in order to pursue my creative work, and it doesn't happen when I'm around other people. I can't predict at all when a creative idea will strike me—it can happen when I'm in the shower, or sitting on the toilet, or lying in bed, or walking around the block. I just know that I have to be alone in order for it to happen.

"Usually I take time for myself in the morning, say between four A.M. and ten A.M. It's really hard to describe what happens, but 'it' happens. What I mean by that is whatever is in my mind just clicks when it is ready to, after all the information and data and reading I have taken in suddenly incubate. I smile to myself because I know that 'it' just happened. I can feel a tingling in my face, I get so excited with what I think I've discovered. I decouple myself from the world—not consciously, but I can't have a conversation with anyone during this time. I can fake it with people, nod my head and say stupid things, but I'm not really there. My body is there, but I left it to go off into my own world."

This physicist has found a way to inject bursts of creative inspiration into his working life. Many other people, who aren't members of professions that allow them to be highly innovative, find ways to improve the quality of their lives through avocational pursuits.

## CREATIVE SIDELINES

A physician I spoke to at length feels his work days are mostly routine. He trained hard to become a doctor, and while he gets considerable satisfaction from his profession, he longs for new challenges. He has found that a sideline as an inventor is a way to improve the quality of his life, and the lives of others, as well as breaking up the monotony of his day-to-day routines:

"The daily practice of medicine is virtually devoid of creativity. People don't realize that the process of diagnosing and treating disease involves very little thought, but is more a matter of applying certain theories or facts to certain situations. Creativity is not encouraged at all in medical training; the emphasis is almost entirely on the acquisition of an overwhelming volume of facts and skills. And once you're out in practice, creativity is even further discouraged by the constant threat of litigation for trying anything the least bit unusual. Things are even more stifling when you consider how structured a doctor's day is, moving from one examining room to the next.

"I feel such a void in my work that I almost had to move into something more creative as a sideline; otherwise, I could never continue to practice medicine without burning out completely. The choice for me to become an inventor was sort of a natural evolution. As a kid I always enjoyed the feeling of solving mathematical or scientific problems. I think it was due, in part, to my need to feel that the world somehow makes sense. It gave me a sense of order and control.

"Inventing is an unusual form of creativity because it involves the combination of complex theoretical principles with highly intuitive thinking. It requires an unusual personality in that first you have to be obsessive in the way you make yourself an expert in a particular field. Then, you have to be real flexible and loose in the way you think up unique ways to use materials that have never been tried before. That's the fun part—the actual creation of an idea, and then following through with its production. For that, you have to be compulsive again, since an invention is of little value to anyone unless it is successfully sold to the public. To do that, I have to deal with patent attorneys as well as manufacturing and marketing experts. Although thinking of a new invention is incredibly rewarding in itself, the same way that composing music or sculpting is rewarding, an enduring feeling of success is gained only after others can use what I've created."

He stresses that his determination is just as important as his creative ideas. He does find enormous satisfaction in advancing scientific knowledge through his inventions, but most of his motivation to create comes from personal sources. Inventing provides a legitimate opportunity to escape tedious responsibilities. He likes having a ready excuse for taking a day off from work or for taking time away from his family in order to spend quiet time in his study. He feels a certain amount of guilt in doing things for himself, and his life is guided by "shoulds"—he *should* be attending to his patients, he *should* be spending more time with his family. Inventing things is his way of justifying to others that he isn't malingering when he spends time by himself in creative thought.

## EXPRESSIONS OF INDIVIDUALITY

A sixty-six-year-old grandmother has devoted her life to taking care of her numerous children and grandchildren. Bright and talented, she long ago passed up many career opportunities to focus on nurturing others. She has pretty much lived her life vicariously through the accomplishments of her successful husband, brothers, sons and daughters, and grandchildren. While immensely proud of her family's productivity, she nevertheless has harbored a life-long avocation: painting. She feels that her paintings are her unique contribution to the world:

"In the beginning, it gave me pleasure and satisfaction to realize that I could reproduce the things that I saw through my hands. However, as life itself unfolded and living became more complicated and the demands on my time increased and became more compelling, so did the need for me to have privacy, both physically and emotionally. My artwork provides this haven. Time spent creating is a safety valve and release for tensions. I can finish a stint of painting feeling totally exhausted by the effort and equally refreshed by the change. I am more ready to face the demands of reality again. I feel relieved for having gone back to one of my resources for sustenance. If this sounds dramatic, it's because it feels that way to me.

"Empty canvas is unexplored territory. What I can create is totally mine. No one else has ever, or will ever, do the portrait or still life or landscape as I am doing it. Talk about privacy, this is the ultimate! What could be more personal than the act of creation?

"I become so totally immersed in the process that frequently I do not hear people speak to me or the telephone ringing. To me the act of creating is more important than the result that I produce. I stop when I have made my statement. After assessing the relative merits of a work, I lose the interest in it that sustained me while I was working on it. I'm told this happens to many, if not all, creators— that is, it's the process that is important, not the result. All I wish to do is progress in my work, to learn from what I have done before."

This woman describes eloquently the rewards of creative solitude. While it is indeed satisfying to examine proudly the cake you've baked, the flowers you've planted, the sweater you've knitted, or the poem you've written, the act of creation is singularly fulfilling for its own sake. The following story involves one man who found his own unique way to express his individuality through creative activities.

Ralph, an office worker, is normally not very good with his hands—he claims he can barely operate a toaster. He has always been intimidated by tasks that require manual dexterity or aesthetic taste. He delayed for years before purchasing his first home because he was overwhelmed by the prospect of anything needing repair. It was therefore completely out of character for Ralph to attempt the massive project of building a stone wall around his property:

"To somebody else, I guess, it wouldn't seem like a big deal. You know, you slap on some mortar, place the rock down on top, and there you have it. But for me it was like scaling Mount Everest. I had to learn all about stone structures. I visited quarries and studied different kinds of stone. I talked with guys who do this kind of thing for a living, and I started to feel more and more overwhelmed. But I stuck with it. And I was amazed at my long-dormant talent for spotting the right rock for the right place. You have to consider size, color, texture, and weight. After a while, the stones would almost talk to me. I could feel which ones belonged in which parts of the wall.

"I worked on that baby, on and off, for more than a year. It might be the only creative thing I've ever built, at least since second grade. I look out my kitchen window and I see that wall standing there, and I just think to myself: 'Wow, I built that.' Sometimes I can hardly believe it. It's pretty exciting to think that long after I've left this house, probably even after I've left this world, my wall will still be standing."

## TIME ALONE FOR CREATIVITY

Even the most minor hobby can provide tremendous pleasure and satisfaction. Many people find their most precious moments in the throes of discovery or creation. Solitude reaches an apex of intensity and satisfaction during such times. It can make you feel almost like you have redeemed your life through a single act, as if a part of you will live forever because of the unique way in which you contributed something to the world.

However, you need courage and perseverance to follow that creative spirit through. Creativity has a paradoxical nature: you must be playful enough to look at the world with a fresh perspective, yet self-disciplined enough to convert the mere spark of a fantasy into reality. There must be a balance between the analytic logic of the brain's left side and the intuition of the right side, between the qualities of masculine independence and feminine sensitivity, between a reckless sense of mission to overcome obstacles and a view that takes into account the realities of the universe. The one constant that is required for creative acts is a degree of solitude. Without time alone it would be very difficult to reflect on what you think and believe, and discover your own unique ideas.

Your creative spirit can grow during the enjoyment of time alone. Just by letting your imagination roam when you are sitting idle, a number of crazy ideas will pop into your head. Relax. Let it happen. Just let things flow. Forget what other people would think. Never mind the rules. Stay loose and flexible. Trust your own process. If you stay receptive to novel ideas, you will not only have lots of fun, you may create something quite extraordinary.

# 9

# Avoiding Self-Destructive Behaviors

*L*ATE AT NIGHT, while the rest of the city sleeps, a woman in her late thirties sits motionless except for the fingers of her right hand, which are nervously tapping the arm of her chair. Tears run down her cheeks, and the tenseness in her face mars its plain and simple beauty. It is another night like the endless string of those before it, a night without sleep. Her brain refuses to turn off; it keeps racing in idle.

Over and over, she reviews the events of the past months that have forever changed her life. There was a time, not that long ago, when she slept soundly and peacefully next to the husband she had known and loved for sixteen years, the same man who now sleeps next to another woman. No matter how meticulously she remembers their past together, she can find no clues as to how and why things went bad. In the many nights she has sat awake in this chair, she cannot honestly admit she knew anything was wrong at all. She thought they had a perfect marriage. Oh, she heard her husband tease her about being more uninhibited in bed and spending less money—but these were hardly reasons to expect he would leave her.

She looks around the room that is now only half-furnished. The house is so quiet, too quiet whenever the children are staying with their father. Each night she crawls into bed and tries to sleep, but disturbing questions crowd her brain: How will she live? Will she ever trust a man again? What did she do to chase him away? What could she have done differently? Does he ever think about her? How can she go on?

During the day she keeps herself busy, but at night she can't stand to be alone. Even Johnny Carson deserts her when he goes off the air. Now she sits drumming her fingers, waiting for something to happen. It never does. Slowly she rises from her chair, sheds her nightgown and robe until she stands naked and cold on the hard floor. She walks to the stereo, selects several records after careful deliberation, and stacks them on the player. As the loud music blares she begins to dance until time has no meaning. She dances until her body drips with sweat, until her legs and back ache, until the last of the records click off, until she falls in an exhausted heap on the floor. Then she slips uneasily into a shallow and fitful slumber.

## THE DARK SIDE OF SOLITUDE

Private moments clearly have their dark side. There are people, like the woman just described, who spend their time alone engaged in compulsive, self-destructive behaviors. These are people who, because of the stress and conflict in their lives, have lost control of themselves. Any solitary activity that would be perfectly acceptable within the bounds of healthful functioning can run amok for those who can no longer act in moderation. Rather than occasionally treating themselves to a splurge of ice cream, they eat a half-gallon almost every night and then vomit or take laxatives to appease their guilt. Rather than periodically taking a day alone to lie around on the couch, watching television, reading the paper and relaxing, they have thoroughly isolated themselves. They become addicted to their computer screens, their exercise regimens, or their private obsessions. Such people feel they have no choice in how they spend their solitude. Their behavior resembles that of a shrew—a creature that, if isolated under a glass tumbler, will literally eat itself to death, starting with its tail.

What this furry animal and the woman just described have in common is the feeling of being trapped inside one's own body and life circumstances. It is difficult for many people to function in their own company without devouring themselves in stress and internal conflict. The anxiety, depression, loneliness, boredom, and restlessness some people experience in reaction to being alone can cause havoc inside the body. Heart rate, blood pressure, gastric secretions, glandular output, glucose production, respiratory and neurological functioning are severely affected. In fact, every system in the body is impacted by periods of negative aloneness. These are the times of intense isolation and despondency, when it feels as if you are the only person on Earth.

## WHEN BEHAVIOR GOES UNDERGROUND

Isolation sometimes represents a choice on the part of the individual to solve social problems by means of escape. Once separated from the pressures or threats from others that produce intense discomfort, the isolated person may survive, albeit in a limited world. This retreat from social reality can be accomplished through physical separation from others, or through the use of alcohol, drugs, or excessive fantasies. Withdrawal is another way of escaping.

Those instances in which private moments have been taken to an extreme, or when the secret self has become destructive, are often the result of cultural pressures to conform to certain norms. Just as there are people who are constitutionally incapable of accomplishing certain physical feats or intellectual tasks, there are also those who, no matter how hard they try, cannot meet the expectations of

others with regard to certain behaviors. They have trouble
controlling their impulses, and so they act out in privacy
behaviors that ordinarily would be restricted or condemned.

Every known culture, no matter how tolerant, has developed taboos against some behaviors. These can involve sexual conduct (adultery, homosexuality, incest), values (greed,
fraud, heresy), or certain behaviors related to the body.
While society can do a fairly adequate job at stamping out
public displays of deviance, it only succeeds in driving variations from the norm underground.

Sociologists Joseph Bensman and Robert Lilienfeld explain how social repression results in the private distur-
bances we know as neuroses, psychoses, and character
disorders:

> No society has ever fully succeeded in stamping out the
> kinds of behavior, belief, or attributes that it denounces at a
> public level. Thus, individuals emerge whose personalities
> are at odds with the public norms of their society. These
> "deviants," except for psychotics—and even then, not all
> psychotics—know that the public exhibition of their dis-
> cretionary behavior will produce sanctions ranging from
> incarceration or expulsion to the denial of opportunity to
> achieve the best fruits of social position and esteem within
> their society. The consciousness of the disesteem attached to
> deviation from public norms forces them, to the extent that
> they can control their behavior, either to repress its man-
> ifestations or to practice it in secret.

We then have two choices: (1) Don't do anything that
others might disapprove of, or (2) do these things only in
private. In many cases, there is not even the perception of a
choice. Some people, such as the woman at the beginning of
this chapter, feel compelled to engage in acts they feel are
beyond their control. The nature of their disorder is such
that they feel driven to their acts—to overeat, masturbate,
or wash their hands without restraint. They must lie, deceive, hide, mislead, and cover up their activities. In the

same way the body's immunological system protects it from invaders trying to disrupt the equilibrium, human behavior (even dysfunctional behavior) sustains itself by repelling attempts to alter its form.

That is why the nature of psychotherapy must so often be circuitous; we must respect the person's reluctance to change any part of him- or herself for fear of creating an even worse state of affairs. Therapy is usually the last resort after everything else has failed. Either the secret can no longer be kept, the private indulgences are no longer satisfying, or the side effects have become too high a price to pay.

Take the all-too-familiar example of the alcoholic or drug addict. For many years he can maintain a semblance of normalcy to others while "medicating" himself secretly with drugs or alcohol. Yet, eventually, whatever he is hiding from catches up. The body rebels. His behavior becomes erratic and more inappropriate. Loss of job, family, and friends become real possibilities. Yet, the addict's first line of defense is not to change a pattern that is obviously destructive, but to find even more ingenious ways to maintain it. The secret self, no matter how ravaged and under siege, will do anything within its power to resist intrusions. The addict may seek the company of others with a similar affliction (which is why drunks like to hang out together). It is inevitable, however, that all his efforts at denial will fail.

## A LIFE OF SOLITARY EXCESS

As we have seen previously, aloneness is existentially neutral; it simply reflects each person's unique way of expressing his or her individuality in private. Whereas solitude represents the most positive features of being alone (peace and creative energy), loneliness represents the most negative aspects. The term *aloneliness* was coined by educator Tom Kubistant to denote the primary dimension of pathological aloneness. It is composed of equal parts fear (of rejection, vulnerability, intimacy, or failure); anxiety (about performance, dependency, or the aloneness of death); alienation (based on one's beliefs, values, perceptions, attitudes); and isolation (both the feeling within and the reality of social ostracism).

To some extent, all of us experience the symptoms of aloneliness in mild form throughout our lives. Many people feel shame about some of their private behaviors, fearing that they are indicative of some undiagnosed mental problem. It is not unusual to feel apprehensive sometimes while by yourself at night, or to feel doubly anxious when confronted by a conflict when there is nobody else to turn to for support. It is also common to occasionally feel bored, lonely, isolated, separate, and different from the rest of the human race.

You may also experience the symptoms of aloneliness in an intermittent, occasional, and mild form (after a life crisis, for example). However, some people suffer from disorders of aloneliness as a chronic, self-defeating condition. Negative private behavior becomes excessive and self-destructive when it is part of a person's character structure and therefore very difficult to change.

Fred, for example, is attractive but has minimal social experience. In fact, his life is so completely isolated that, at age twenty-six, he has no friends and has never had a date. Although he is extremely lonely, frustrated, and anxious, he feels unable to break through his resistance:

"You are the first person I've talked to in a long time. Besides working in my office, and working out with weights at home, I pretty much keep to myself. I spend almost all my time alone. People have commented to me that they think I'm unfriendly, but it's really just that people make me feel so nervous. So I prefer to be by myself all of the time. I live alone. I eat lunch alone. There are days that can go by without me having to speak to anyone at all. I sort of don't mind all that much.

"I work out a lot in my apartment. I have lots of exercise equipment that fills up my whole apartment; there is barely room for my bed. Every day when I come home from work, I do at least two hours on my free weights or stationary bike or rowing machine. Then I make myself some dinner and spend the evening watching television until I feel tired."

Fred's excessive isolation is one example of how aloneness becomes pathological, when a person has so encapsulated himself into his private world that there is very little social contact. Others pursue a different self-destructive strategy: people who can't tolerate their own company find ways to occupy themselves with internal or external activity so they have no time to feel alone.

## COMPULSIVE STYLES OF SOLITUDE

Some people deal with solitary stress by avoiding aloneness to an extreme. They keep themselves constantly occupied with distractions to avoid dealing with an inner self they find frightening. As long as one is working eighty hours per week or running eighty miles per week, there is neither the time nor the energy to contemplate the emptiness of one's life.

*The workaholic.* One man structures his whole life like the shrew mentioned earlier. He must stay in motion every second of his waking life:

"From the moment my eyes pop open I'm on the run. I keep myself so busy I never have time to think much about myself. I'm at the office every day by seven A.M. and I'm on the phone constantly. Even in my car I have to return calls and make notes to myself. By the time I get home at about seven P.M., I have already organized in my mind what unfinished business I'm going to work on after a quick dinner. I fall into bed about eleven and fall asleep instantly."

Six-and-a-half days a week, fifty-one weeks a year, for

over nine years, this professional has spent most of his life working at this pace. He doesn't need to work this hard for economic or security reasons. He is already a major partner in his firm and has more money than he has time to spend. But as long as he keeps moving, he has no time to think about where he is going and why. He doesn't know his children well, nor does he want to—he finds them self-centered, ungrateful, and spoiled. He considers his marriage a good one in that there are no fights or disagreements. He works; she lunches and shops. The Sunday morning he takes off each week is quite enough to convince him he has made the right choice in spending as much time as he can working by himself, content with his productivity.

*The computer addict.*   A specific subset of workaholic behavior has emerged fairly recently in those who become addicted to a single solitary activity to the exclusion of other facets of life. One example is the subculture of people who are so uncomfortable in the outside world that they have retreated into the solitary world of the computer. These "computer hacks," as they call themselves, grew up alone and prefer to stay that way. The computer becomes a partner—it talks back, responds instantaneously to its user's commands, yet makes no demands in return. It provides a way to avoid intimacy and vulnerability without feeling bored or lonely.

Sherry Turkle has studied the isolated world of the computer addict. Complete "nerds" in the social arena—awkward, shy, inept—computer hackers seek to attain mastery of their machines as a substitute for their social ineptitude. They may spend up to fifteen or twenty hours each day sitting at the keyboard playing with their programs. They take pride in their virtuoso skills. They may not know their way around a lover's body, but they sure know their software.

One of Turkle's subjects, a chemical engineering student at MIT, poignantly describes his attraction to the technological world:

I think of the world as divided between flesh things and machine things. The flesh things have feelings, need you to know them, to take risks, to let yourself go. You never know what to expect of them. And all the things that I was into when I was growing up, well, they were not those kind of things. Math, you could get perfect. Chemistry, you could get exactly the right values when you did your experiments. No risks. I guess I like perfection. I stay away from the flesh things. I think this makes me sort of a nonperson. I often don't feel like a flesh thing myself. I hang around machines, but I hate myself a lot of the time. In a way it's like masturbating. You can always satisfy yourself to perfection. With another person, who knows what might happen? You might get rejected. You might do it wrong. Too much risk. You can see why I'm not too pleased with the way my personality turned out.

Computer hackers who find solace and safety in their machines are not the only computer addicts. Thousands of others live in the fantasy world of video games. In just a decade, the level of sophistication moved from Pong, a relatively primitive video game, to the seductive Pac Man, which captured the lunch hours of school kids and business people around the world, to the present Nintendo craze. Once these games moved out of the arcade and into individual personal computers and TV sets, the amount of solitary time logged on the joystick multiplied accordingly. Now there are interactive fiction games that require a commitment of several hundred hours. Participants stay glued to their screens as they travel to a dead planet inhabited only by a robot named Floyd.

Whether destroying wicked aliens or reliving the Battle of the Bulge, the computer provides more than harmless entertainment and diversion for those who are comfortable only in their aloneness. When they feel bored, lonely, or agitated and long for companionship, some people find it much easier to simply flip a switch than to initiate contact with others.

*The exercise fanatic.* Similar patterns emerge with the compulsive exerciser as with the workaholic. While research has indicated that exercising about twenty minutes three times per week is sufficient to produce desired gains in cardiovascular and physical fitness, some people go far beyond this. Some runners, bicyclists, aerobic exercisers, swimmers, weight lifters, and cross-country skiers devote up to three hours every day to strenuous workouts. This level of activity can hardly be justified on the grounds of improving one's body. Such individuals, in fact, are often plagued by injury, their bodies breaking down from steady overuse.

The reasons why people exercise compulsively and excessively have nothing to do with the body, but rather with the experience of being or feeling alone. One surgeon, who wakes up every morning at five to train for the ultra-marathons he runs, realizes all too well that his activity has little to do with feeling fit—especially since he is chronically injured with stress fractures and tendinitis. He is so controlled by his need to work off stress that he ran the Boston Marathon with a disintegrated vertebra. But pain is part of the package—there is something heroic about subjecting yourself to this sort of abuse and proving you can take it.

It is easy for this doctor to be alone when he has something to do, especially when it is an activity that stifles heavy thinking with endorphin overload:

"I run not because I want to, but because I have to. Years ago I sprained my ankle and had to stay off my feet for a few days. It was a nightmare. I was bouncing off walls. Couldn't sleep. I gained five pounds. I was just a wreck. I don't run for the exercise, but just to keep myself wired together. The more I run, the calmer and more in control I feel. I know I overdo it [he runs twelve to eighteen miles per day] but, what the heck, it beats smoking pot [as he used to do before running]. When I'm out there on the road I feel invincible. Nobody else can get to me. The world just shuts off. It's too bad the runs have to end. . . ."

*Eating disorders.*   There are many similarities between the compulsive exerciser or workaholic and those with eating disorders or other obsessive styles. Just as obligatory runners can literally run themselves to death, so can the anorexic or bulimic starve herself to death (women suffer eating disorders at a much higher rate than men)—all in pursuit of an "ideal" body image.

Also noteworthy in the bulimic is a distinctly dysfunctional way of being alone. Reed Larson and social scientists at the University of Chicago studied the unique pattern of solitude characteristic of those with bulimia. They found that while these people may be able to handle time alone at work quite well, unstructured private moments cause them great discomfort. Being alone, with its problems of impulse control and the need to be secretive, induces guilt and stress. Gorging on food is sometimes the only thing that brings temporary relief, as described by this college student:

"I don't have any control over myself. I can't help it. It just happens. Once every day, usually after lunch or dinner, I sneak away to the bathroom. I figure out the exact time that I can be alone long enough that nobody can hear me. Halfway through dinner I start a dialogue in my head: Do I want to throw up? How will it feel? Can I get away with it? I drink a glass of water just in case I might want to vomit later. You have to drink a lot of water to make it come out easily.

"It's this big secret that I've kept from my family and friends for such a long time. Nobody knows I do this. I guess that's part of the thrill. It's such a challenge to avoid being caught. There's so much planning that goes into it."

*The obsessive-compulsive.*   In all of these cases, and the ones to follow, the person attempts to manage stress and

internal strife that grow worse during private moments by
narrowly focusing attention on a single goal or theme. This
is certainly true of another chronic style of disturbed aloneness, in which the obsessive-compulsive uses rituals to
structure solitary time. In this condition an idea or impulse
repetitively and persistently invades a person's consciousness, usually accompanied with the dread of some impending disaster. The person has little control over these
impulses; indeed they seem not to be part of the self.
Efforts to resist the intrusions only create further anxiety
and frustration, thus occupying all of one's conscious awareness when alone until it is virtually impossible to think
about anything else. In his memoirs, English writer George
Borrow describes an encounter with one such fellow who
attempted to stave off disaster through the magical thinking
of the obsessive-compulsive:

> There was one thing that I loved better than the choicest gift
> which could be bestowed upon me, better than life itself—
> my mother; at length she became unwell, and the thought
> that I might possibly lose her now rushed into my mind for
> the first time; it was terrible, and caused me unspeakable
> misery, I may say horror. My mother became worse, and I was
> not allowed to enter her apartment, lest by my frantic ex-
> clamations of grief I might aggravate her disorder. I rested
> neither day nor night, but roamed about the house like one
> distracted. Suddenly I found myself doing that which even at
> the time struck me as being highly singular; I found myself
> touching particular objects that were near me, and to which
> my fingers seemed to be attracted by an irresistible impulse.
> It was now the table or the chair that I was compelled to
> touch; now the bell-rope, now the handle of the door; now
> I would touch the wall, and the next moment stooping down, I
> would place the point of my finger upon the floor; and so
> I continued to do day after day; frequently I would struggle
> to resist the impulse, but invariably in vain. I have even
> rushed away from the object, but I was sure to return, the
> impulse was too strong to be resisted: I quickly hurried back,

compelled by the feeling within me to touch the object. Now, I need not tell you that what impelled me to these actions was the desire to prevent my mother's death; whenever I touched any particular object, it was with the view of baffling the evil chance, as you would call it—in this instance my mother's death.

It has been estimated that more than 4 million people in the United States engage in private compulsive rituals they are powerless to stop. They may be repetitive hand washers, obsessively preoccupied with thoughts of contamination, aggression, or sex, compulsive hoarders, counters, or organizers. In her book on the subject of obsessive-compulsive disorders, Judith Rapoport comments that one feature shared by the afflicted is the ability to act as if they are normal—to display public success in the midst of a private hell.

*Superstitious behavior.* On a much more moderate level, most of us can relate to those involuntary compulsive behaviors that often take the form of superstitious rituals. For example, during the anticipation of some significant event—perhaps driving to an important meeting, date, or interview—one might interpret events, such as the changing of a stoplight or the appearance of a particular license plate or type of vehicle, as a sign as to how things will work out.

In some individuals, superstitious rituals take on a compulsive pattern:

"When I'm alone I like to stay busy. I do some heavy-duty cleaning around the house. I wash windows, wax the floor, clean the walls. Some people would say I'm a bit compulsive. I suppose that's true. When friends open a drawer in my house they go crazy—all the pencils are arranged according to size, everything is ordered perfectly symmetrical. Sometimes I will do things like alphabetize the spice rack or soup cans on the shelf. It feels like as long as I can organize my house like this, my life will stay in control.

But if something gets out of place, maybe my life will come apart, too. I would never tell anyone about my little quirks; they'd think I'm nuts or something."

This woman's behavior may seem a bit excessive, but her belief in superstitious rituals is not unusual. We are not surprised to see buildings with no floor 13, planes with no row 13, or train stations with no gate 13. We don't raise an eyebrow when someone "knocks on wood," avoids stepping on a crack, crosses herself, or jumps for joy after catching a bride's bouquet. But there are many other superstitious rituals that we engage in only when we are alone. Upon entering his car, one man always completes a series of actions designed to prevent an accident (although he admits his behavior is ridiculous). His dilemma occurs when he has a passenger next to him and he must surreptitiously hum a particular tune while pressing the brakes three times, start the car without touching the steering wheel, and push the rear-view mirror up so he will not accidentally catch a reflected glimpse of himself. "That's why," he explains, "I always make somebody else drive."

If all of this seems a bit strange to you, consider whether your own solitary rituals include any of the following:

- Wearing particular articles of clothing or carrying a special object for good luck.
- Avoiding certain places or times that have previously brought unfortunate results.
- Reciting a prayer or motto before attempting a difficult task.
- Reading your horoscope or fortune cookie, laughing out loud at its absurdity, and then taking due care to follow its prescription.
- Wishing for something you really want while blowing out birthday candles.
- Repeating exactly the same sequence of actions that brought good luck before.

Superstitions are usually described as irrational behaviors, based upon fear or ignorance, that are designed to offer protection against the unknown or mysterious. When faced with circumstances beyond their control, people will try to gain whatever edge they can. Habits such as the use of lucky charms give people some sense of security and a feeling of being powerful. Even well-educated, logical types will shrug at their "illogical" beliefs in charms or magic with the confession that even if such things don't help, they certainly don't hurt.

## INVOLUNTARY ISOLATION FROM OTHERS

Up to this point in this chapter we've looked at people who can't tolerate unstructured time alone very well. Now we turn to those who choose to spend time in their own company because of an inability to establish intimate relationships. For some people who can't or won't function in the world of others, being alone is the only alternative. Such unhappy individuals feel exiled against their will. The following words, spoken by a young man who has all but given up interacting with other people, represents those who experience aloneness to an extreme.

"Since I was four years old, I've felt completely alone in the world. I never liked myself, nor felt I deserved to be in the world of others. As a child I was constantly injuring myself—falling through glass doors, falling out of trees, falling off my bike—all probably accidentally on purpose. I've always had recurring nightmares—the screaming kind—so even sleep is no escape for me. I try to get through each day in five-minute increments.

"One theme that has remained stable throughout my life is the avoidance of being around other people. I just prefer to be alone. As a child, I never wanted to celebrate my birthdays because I didn't want to draw any attention to myself. Even as an adult, I have never celebrated my birthday, nor even told anyone when it is.

"It is very important for me to be able to control and structure every aspect of my life because I feel so vulnerable much of the time. Because I can *only* do that when I'm alone and away from unpredictable situations and insensitive people, I prefer to be alone all the time. Sure, it's uncomfortable sometimes. But *that* I've learned to live with."

People like this man have trouble forming relationships. They appear withdrawn, reclusive, unresponsive, and show little warmth or compassion. We might almost wonder whether "anybody is at home" inside the person, since he displays little emotional reaction to anything. Another remarkable feature of such a person (often diagnosed as a "schizoid personality") is that, while usually friendless and isolated, he experiences little loneliness or boredom. The only thing that might upset him is any disruption in his reclusive routine that forces him to interact with others. As you might imagine, the prognosis for this illness of aloneliness is poor. Eighty percent of children who manifest these symptoms of disinterest and avoidance of others maintain this pattern throughout life. Another 10 percent eventually graduate to a full-blown schizophrenic process.

What causes some people to exhibit such isolating tendencies? It is suspected that both genetic structure and environment play a part. Those infants who show an early tendency to withdraw, who are oversensitive to strangers, who are exposed to limited social contact and unpredictable parental separations, seem to be at greater risk. The symptoms develop as the young child, already fearful and vulnerable to rejection, retreats into the self during some developmental crisis.

There are individuals such as the schizoid who appear to care less whether they form any relationships or not. But the majority of those who are involuntarily isolated feel great dissatisfaction. One relatively common example of this is the case of shyness. Shy people avoid human contact most of the time because of disabling terror.

In a study of three hundred "love shy" men who had never had a close, romantic relationship, sociologist Brian Gilmartin found that the great majority had been bullied in childhood. It appears as if early social rejection or harassment leaves enduring scars in the personalities of some, who later cannot muster the confidence to approach others.

Perhaps the best description of shyness in an extreme and chronic form is presented by Phillip Zimbardo in his book on the subject:

> I remember as far back as 4 years old, some of the stuff I used to do to avoid seeing people that came to visit us. They were people I knew, like cousins, aunts, uncles, friends of the family, and even my brothers and sister. I hid in clothes baskets, hampers, closets, in sleeping bags, under beds and there's an endless list, all because I was scared of people.
>
> As I grew up, things got worse.

Zimbardo has found that 40 percent of people label themselves as "shy," a condition that involves a lack of confidence, a deficiency in social skills, feelings of intimidation or awkwardness in group settings, fear of interpersonal risk, and more time spent alone than is preferred. Most of all, shy people stay isolated because of intense self-consciousness, a tendency to repeat inhibiting internal messages such as the childhood lament: "Nobody likes me. Everybody hates me." Other internally based messages that promote continued withdrawal include: "I'm too fat." "These people are much better than I am." "What if I say something stupid?" "I'll probably have a lousy time anyway." "Everybody is noticing how uncomfortable I am."

The fear of showing one's feelings to others, of not being able to control the display of awkwardness in such symptoms as stuttering or blushing, causes further problems in overcoming shyness. Ironically, some people can break out

of their shyness for specific performances. Many public fig-
ures—writers, artists, politicians, actors, athletes—are prime
examples. Entertainer Michael Jackson perhaps epitomizes
this phenomenon: on stage he projects an image of the most
dynamic, self-assured, social human being on Earth, yet
once the performance ends he lives almost as a recluse,
painfully shy and uncomfortable around others.

Many people never outgrow the insecurities and shyness
of their adolescent years. They continue to feel crippled by
fears, apprehensions, and anxiety, so they have chosen an
existence that is lonely but predictable, boring but safe,
painful but secure. It is difficult for them to realize that
whatever terrible things they think might occur if they were
to reach out beyond their walls of self-protection, they
could not possibly be worse than the feelings of loneliness.

## STEPS TO CHANGING
## SELF-DESTRUCTIVE BEHAVIOR

Private moments stimulate stress and conflict in people's
lives when they are taken to an extreme. Unless you are one
of those rare people born without the capacity for connecting with others, you can improve the quality of your private
moments without sacrificing the intimacy in your relationships. Most of the self-destructive behaviors mentioned
in this chapter—obsessions, compulsions, addictions, social
withdrawal, shyness, aloneliness—are amenable to treatment.

When your own efforts at reading, studying, and prod-
ding yourself to try thinking and acting differently are not
enough, a qualified professional can help you learn to
change habitual self-destructive patterns. Although the variety of therapeutic approaches is staggering (over three hundred at latest count), there are certain common elements to
which the majority of mental-health experts subscribe.

I have combined the best features of several therapeutic

methodologies into a cognitive process that you can follow in working through a number of unresolved personal issues. For each of these seventeen steps, which are part of any systematic effort to change, I have presented several questions to ask yourself, and then illustrated the points with a case example (in italics) of how one man might apply the process. This man has a difficult time tolerating his own company for very long, a situation he would like to rectify.

1. *Articulate the reasons why you want to change.* Why now? What in your life isn't working any longer? What has changed recently to make it more difficult for you to maintain your dysfunctional behavior?

*I hate being alone. I didn't realize just how much I dread my own company until I spent an extended weekend by myself because my family went out of town. To make matters even worse, there was a terrible ice storm that knocked out all the electricity and stranded me in the house for twenty-four hours. No phones. No television. No radio. I went nuts!*

2. *Formulate clear goals and expectations of where you would like to be in your life.* After you have completed work on yourself, what progress would you like to make in specific areas? What goals do you long for that are both realistic and attainable?

*I would like to get to the point where I can feel more comfortable in my own company without having to resort to constant distractions and diversions.*

3. *Identify sources of resistance that may interfere with your efforts to change.* Who in your life has a vested interest in keeping you the way you are? What are you aware of inside you that is working to sabotage your self-improvement work?

*I know my wife may be threatened by this expression of my independence and need for more freedom. More to the point, I*

*feel real reluctant to change this aspect of my life—maybe if I
spent time in solitude I will start considering some things I am
doing in my life that I don't like. It may start a chain reaction.*

4. Conduct a thorough self-assessment of those aspects of your functioning that are self-destructive.
What behaviors are getting in the way of what you want in
life? What aspects of your thoughts, feelings, responses,
values, and behavioral patterns are less effective than they
could be?

*I am so limited in my behaviors, so impaired in my ability to
do things on my own. I am constantly searching for companions
and company to do things because I don't have the courage and
motivation to do them myself.*

5. Explore the source of these difficulties within
the context of your personal history.   What is familiar
about this problem that you have experienced before in
your life? What influences from your past have helped
create these problems?

*A number of things come to mind: I remember being afraid as
a kid when I was by myself, and my parents usually indulged
me—they thought it was cute. Also, I've never thought of myself
as a very deep thinker, so I tended to avoid situations when I
would have to face how stupid I might really be.*

6. Discover hidden and unconscious motives behind
your self-defeating behaviors.   What sustains their continued existence? What advantages are you accruing as a
result of being this way?

*As long as I stay busy and have others around me, I feel
reassured and safe. I also have a great excuse for not experimenting with new activities since I tell myself it's not my style.*

7. Express pent-up frustrations and other feelings
about what you are experiencing.   How are you feeling
about all of this? How are you dealing with your anger,

your resentments, your fears, your loneliness, and your dis-
couragement?

*This feels real scary for me to be getting into this whole area.
I'm also aware of the resentments I still hold onto—especially
toward my mother for being so needy that she smothered me, and
toward my father for allowing me to become so dependent. This
task of changing this lifelong pattern feels overwhelming!*

**8. Mobilize a support system to offer encourage-
ment and nurturance.** Who in your life can you really
trust to help you? Who feels safe enough to reach out to?

*I think my wife would be supportive of what I want to do if I
shared with her what I am feeling and where I am coming from. I
have a few friends who could be of help as well—they are already
good at enjoying their solitude and I bet they could give me some
hints.*

**9. Challenge assumptions that are ineffective.** What
irrational or illogical beliefs do you hold that are gross exaggerations of reality? Which values or thinking patterns
are obsolete, given the new person you wish to be?

*My greatest fear is: What if I'm making a mistake by opening
up this whole can of worms? I'm also aware of a lot of negative
thinking on my part—that I will probably fail, that I won't like
the new person I want to be, that my wife will probably desert
me because she will feel neglected, that I'm being selfish by even
considering doing some things on my own.*

**10. Confront inconsistencies in your thinking and
behavior.** What discrepancies are there between what you
say, what you feel, and what you think? How can you challenge your irrational thinking?

*I realize, of course, that by forging ahead with this commit-
ment I could very well be in for some difficult times. But I don't
see another way out. And furthermore, even if I was making a
mistake (which I doubt very seriously), it won't be the first time.*

*I have rarely regretted things I've tried; mostly I've regretted things I* haven't *done.*

**11. Renew a commitment to follow through on the hard work of changing a core aspect of your existence.**  Based on what you now understand, are you prepared to accept responsibility for following through on a plan of action?

*I don't have as much choice as I think I do. There is no way I can continue living my life the way I am and avoiding dealing with my unresolved stuff. It is absurd that a man my age still avoids being alone! It affects so many other areas of my life that I plan my whole schedule around keeping myself busy so I don't have to be "stuck" in my own company. I've got to carry this through wherever it may lead!*

**12. Formulate a plan.**  Given what you say you want, how can you obtain it? What do you need to do to meet your goals?

*First, I should explain to my family and friends what I am attempting so I can enlist their support. Then, I should start spending short periods of time alone, gradually increasing my tolerance. Most importantly, I need to pay attention to what thoughts and feelings come up for me as a result of these experiments.*

**13. Go beyond your existing comfort zone.**  What risks can you take to try acting differently in situations in which you would normally play it safe? What can you do to stir up some constructive excitement?

*Most of what I have to do is to counteract the excuses I give myself for not following through on this. I need to push myself into new territory. Eventually, I would like to work up to a camping trip alone. Time to just be by myself . . . and with myself.*

*14. Solicit constructive feedback.* Do other people perceive a difference in you? Whom can you ask to tell you honestly and straightforwardly any changes they have seen?

*A number of people have already reported that they have seen a change in me. I seem more alive, more engaged in life. Yet, I have also heard that in some ways I appear more preoccupied. I have to be cautious to not take this solitude too far, to the point where I neglect the people who are most important to me.*

*15. Conduct a thorough evaluation of your progress.* Are you moving closer to the way you wish to be? How are things going so far?

*I feel like things are moving right on schedule. As much as I would like to know how this will all turn out, I am excited about the ways I already feel different. At least I don't feel helpless and complacent any longer—I am doing something to change my life and make it better.*

*16. Generalize results.* How can you apply what you have learned to other areas of your life? How is this issue you have been working on similar to other unresolved problems?

*This one issue of feeling afraid of my own company, and facing myself when I'm alone, is certainly the biggest struggle of my life. Yet, it is related to most other problems in my life—my avoidance of changing jobs because of a reluctance to leave co-workers I have grown up with, my need to hold on to friendships I have outgrown just so I can have company, even the dependencies I foster in other relationships with my family. By working on this one theme, I can try to get closer to resolving all the others.*

*17. Maintain the progress.* What do you need to do to minimize the chance of setbacks? How can you continue working on this area of yourself in the future?

*I must first realize that setbacks are inevitable. No matter how*

*much I plan and try to anticipate every contingency, progress will*
*continue in a sporadic fashion. I have to realize, however, that as*
*long as I keep working on myself, confronting my fears directly*
*rather than continuing old patterns, eventually I will get to the*
*place where I want to be.*

While this particular example dealt with a man who was
afraid of his private moments, the same process could as
easily be applied to the opposite theme—a person who
spends so much time alone that he isolates himself from
others. In both instances, and in any other issue you may
wish to resolve, you have to identify the specific problem,
explore its parameters, and target a program that breaks the
cycle of inertia that is so much a part of self-defeating
conduct. Between these two polarities of solitude deprivation and excessive isolation is an existence that contains
both enriched interpersonal relationships and meaningful
private moments. Such a balance is not only possible, but
with sufficient motivation and practice, is well within your
grasp.

# 10

# *Mastering the Art of Being Alone*

*I*T HAS BEEN primarily solitary personalities who have changed the world. Those who are skilled at being alone, who know how to entertain and occupy themselves, and who celebrate their solitude have made the most significant contributions to humankind. When necessary, such individuals seem to be relatively impervious to the scorn others show toward their seemingly bizarre ideas. They develop an immunity to social dependence and approval, and they find a way to convert periods of isolation into spurts of productivity.

Throughout history, solitary individuals such as Moses, Jesus, Buddha, Socrates, and Confucius have retreated into isolation to reach clarity and enlightenment. In more recent times, luminaries such as Sigmund Freud, Albert Einstein, and Emily Dickinson drew strength from their social exile to create singular works. Other famous lives were also steeped in aloneness: Lincoln, Spinoza, Dostoyevsky, Cervantes, Tolstoy, Wagner, Nietzsche, Rousseau, Saint Augustine, Montaigne, Ibsen, Tchaikovsky, Martin Luther.

What all of these great people had in common was a desire to make being alone the significant priority of their lives. They taught themselves to convert any negative feelings of loneliness and alienation into avenues of revelation about themselves and others. They perceived their pain as having an underlying purpose: to intensify their sensitivity to things around them and to transform their energy into creative channels.

## PORTALS OF DISCOVERY

The feeling of aloneness is never an absolute condition; rather, it is relative to the dimension of "otherness" you feel in the connection to people you love. As philosopher Fred Kersten remarked, "One is always alone with or among things and others." During times of fellowship, a part of you stands alone, separate from all that happens around you. Similarly, during periods of intense isolation, there is always a part of you interconnected to the others of your past and present.

In his treatise on the relationship between loneliness and solitude, Kersten points out that both experiences are actually modes of discovery—not only of yourself, but also of the world you inhabit. "For that reason the self is always capable of experience and action—that is to say, is never isolated. Loneliness and solitude therefore discover rather than conceal the world, self, others, and things."

The paradox of private moments is that your secret self allows you to be without others even in their presence, or with others even in their absence. The important part of this equation is that *the choice is yours;* you determine how you feel. Your experience depends on how you interpret its meaning. When any pain associated with aloneness is perceived to have some underlying purpose, private time becomes a portal of discovery about self and others.

Existential therapists such as Viktor Frankl believe the creation of personal meaning is central to a satisfying life. This is not simply the a priori pronouncement of an academic armchair philosopher musing about life's mysteries. Frankl did not create his philosophy in the halls of Harvard or Stanford, but behind the barbed wire in Auschwitz, where he was interned for years watching his family and friends perish. A psychiatrist by training, Frankl observed that whether people lived or died seemed to depend, more than anything else, on the meaning they gave to their suffer-

ing—even if they were determined to survive only to tell
the world about their plight:

> We who lived in concentration camps can remember the men
> who walked through the huts comforting others, giving away
> their last piece of bread. They may have been few in number,
> but they offer sufficient proof that everything can be taken
> from a man but one last thing: the last of the human free-
> doms—to choose one's attitude in any given set of circum-
> stances, to choose one's own way. . . . Even though condi-
> tions such as lack of sleep, insufficient food and various
> mental stresses may suggest that the inmates were bound to
> react in certain ways, in the final analysis it becomes clear
> that the sort of person the prisoner became was the result of
> an inner decision, and not the result of camp influences
> alone. Fundamentally, therefore, any man can, even under
> such circumstances, decide what shall become of him—
> mentally and spiritually. He may retain his human dignity
> even in a concentration camp.

If it is possible to endure the suffering of the concentration camp with one's dignity intact, it is certainly feasible to
do the same about any unpleasant or difficult aspects of
being alone. Nobody has stolen your freedom; you voluntarily relinquished it. No one has placed you in prison; you
have trapped yourself in isolation through the avoidance of
responsibility for your own existence. As philosopher Jean-
Paul Sartre has remarked: "It is therefore senseless to think
of complaining since nothing foreign has decided what we
feel, what we live, or what we are."

## CHOOSING TO BE ALONE

While you most certainly had no choice about whether to
be born, once thrown into the world you *are* responsible for
everything you do and feel. You may be unable or unwilling to alter your marital status, living situation, or other

circumstances of existence, but you can choose to accept responsibility for how you *feel* about your time alone and how you use it.

If I begin to experience a certain restlessness after some hours of uninterrupted isolation, leading to jitters and eventually to a high degree of anxiety while considering an unresolved issue in my life, I have several options. I can, of course, summarily stifle my discomfort by ending the isolation; once I rejoin the world of others I will be sufficiently distracted by my obligations to have no further time for disturbing thoughts. I may, however, wish to extend my private time without prolonging my suffering. I can do this if I can deal effectively with what is bothering me. This can involve a dialogue with myself, including direct confrontation with the issues I have been avoiding. By staying with my feelings, exploring their substance and form, checking out their origins, disputing their irrational roots, acknowledging that which I can't (or won't) control, eventually I reach a truce that allows me to continue on my solitary path. I no longer feel ambushed, but simply nudged to deal with unfinished business.

Loneliness is felt most deeply by those who have abandoned hope, relinquished responsibility, neglected freedom, and sentenced themselves to a life without choices. In this sense, loneliness can become a portal of discovery about yourself, the world, and the relationship between the two when you strive toward growth and understanding. In fact, nothing in life that is accomplished with pride ever comes without a certain degree of hardship, aggravation, or risk. This is true of bearing and raising children, beginning or ending a relationship, changing jobs, or attempting any new endeavor.

As I have discussed through this book, solitude is a particular kind of aloneness that is distinct from other modes—loneliness, isolation, privacy, alienation, withdrawal, or even silence. Further, it is not the condition of a person at rest, but a state of stillness and quiet characterized by active contemplation. It is a state of attentiveness and presence in the private moment that facilitates an emergence of integration and wholeness. Essayist Oliver Morgan underscores the meaning of solitude as a condition that is almost always an expression of free will:

> Solitude is a choice. It is a willing decision to allow the longing for quiet to have its due, its rightful place and time in one's life. It is a willingness to allow the everyday and distracting to recede, and to allow the silence to envelop one like sleep. It is a decision to permit solitude to take hold and become a disclosure experience from deep within. Solitude is a way of being with oneself, of learning to endure oneself, of becoming comfortable with the mystery that is one's Self. Solitude is a decision to encounter one's inner Self, and only decision allows it to become part of one's lifestyle.

Since one of the characteristics that distinguishes solitude from negative forms of aloneness is the exercise of free choice, it is imperative to our emotional well-being that we devote considerable time to developing this internal capacity. This is most readily accomplished by making quality private moments more of a priority in our lives, and especially by following the suggestion below from theologian K. Rahner:

> Have the courage to be alone . . . for once try to endure your own company for a while. Perhaps you can find a room where you can be alone. Or you may know a lonely walk or a quiet church. Don't speak, then, not even with yourself nor with the others with whom we dispute and quarrel even when they are not there. Wait. Listen . . . Endure yourself!

## THE FUTURE OF SOLITUDE

I mentioned previously that the skills of enjoying solitude will become more crucial for life satisfaction in the future. The past century has seen a dramatic decline in those social structures that supported a sense of belongingness. Interest in formal religion has been steadily waning, as has commitment to a community. With the invention of air conditioning, people spend more time indoors, insulated from their neighbors. Houses are no longer erected with front porches for sitting, and subdivision life is devoid of sidewalks. Doctors no longer make house calls. Local drugstores and grocery stores have long since been gobbled up by large, impersonal chain operations. Corporate relocations have scattered extended families across the globe. This progress has created greater material comfort and convenience, but at the expense of increased anonymity and isolation.

The inclination of people to spend time alone, indeed the social freedom to do so, is a relatively new historical event. According to historian Philip Aries: "Until the end of the 17th century, nobody was ever left alone. The density of social life made isolation virtually impossible." Not too long ago one had little choice but to spend all of one's time in the company of others—family members, neighbors, people one liked and often people one did not like. In most households the entire family, if not several generations, lived together in a single room. Every action and change of behavior was observed and often commented upon. No one's thoughts and feelings were his own.

In the last few hundred years we have come to grant a right to privacy and solitude to people other than monks, shepherds, and outlaws. This is possible for a number of reasons, most notably that our society is more stable and thus more tolerant of individual differences. Values have also evolved to put a greater emphasis on individual rights, equal opportunity, freedom, independence, creativity, and privacy. This trend toward spending more time alone is continuing.

During the last twenty years, the number of people choosing to live alone has increased dramatically. From college students to single and divorced adults, to the widowed elderly, people are electing to live by themselves. The percentage of the elderly in our society is growing three times as fast as the total population—in some countries it will soon reach 20 percent. In North America and Europe the divorce rate continues to rise, creating growing numbers of single-adult households. In addition, there is a growing proliferation of highly seductive forms of passive entertainment, such as television, video-tape players, books on audio tape, stereos, computers—all to make time spent alone more appealing.

Today, most people enjoy greater affluence than their parents did at a similar stage in life. We have greater means and opportunity to spend time alone. We enjoy a shorter and less physically tiring work week due to skyrocketing technology. We have fewer social obligations. Considering all these factors, it is likely that living with solitude will indeed be a primary life skill of the future. If this is so, then we would all be well advised to increase our tolerance for private moments and improve our abilities to make the most of this time. Like any set of underdeveloped skills, with determination and systematic practice you too can master the art of being alone.

## THE ART OF BEING ALONE

Based on my research, I have identified several qualities that are consistently present in those who are highly proficient at making the most of their private moments. Such experts in solitude demonstrate the following qualities:

*An appreciation for what solitude can provide.* Solitude is a primary way of developing inner resources and increasing your powers of intuition and independence. It is a source of inspiration, productivity, and self-entertainment.

*A release of inhibition, shame, and guilt.* Spending time alone permits you the opportunity to become comfortable with yourself in the most natural state possible. Through practice and concerted efforts, you eventually learn to accept yourself as you are.

*An ability to think positively.* People who are good at being alone have a unique way of talking to themselves inside their heads that is distinctly different from those who feel lonely or anxious during solitude. They are able to change the way they feel about their aloneness by altering many of their internal messages to emphasize self-control and personal choice. They try to avoid negative self-statements by substituting more positive ones. For example: "Nobody put me in this life situation; I did it to myself, so I can pull myself out of it when I'm ready," rather than "I'm stuck and there's nothing I can do about it."

*A support system of others who are tolerant of the need to be alone.* People have a strong desire, if not a need, to keep a part of their lives private, even from those they love and trust the most. Since family members and friends may sometimes disapprove of your interest in solitary activities because it takes time away from them, it is very important that you strike a balance between remaining sensitive to others' needs and meeting your own. It takes time and effort to teach others to respect your privacy. I recall a woman who, although part of a very loving and nurturing family, felt periodic urges to go off by herself for several hours each week. If her husband and children interfered with this solitude, she noticed herself becoming progressively more restless and resentful. She found that the art of being alone involved more than being able to enjoy her own company; of equal importance was her ability to teach others around her to respect this private time without feeling threatened or neglected.

*The courage to face yourself without distractions.*
Being alone means confronting the restlessness inside you.
It means increasing your threshold for tolerating frustration, boredom, and inner turmoil. In gradually larger doses,
you are able to spend prolonged periods alone without feeling the need to escape from yourself, from your fears, your
loneliness, your unresolved life issues.

*A willingness to experiment with new ways of being
and to initiate activities in a proactive fashion.* The art
of being alone involves not waiting to be entertained but
creating your own diversions. It means not settling into
predictable routines but creating new, more interesting behavior patterns. It requires not avoiding constructive risks,
but exploring the unknown whenever possible. Instead of
blaming others for dissatisfactions you experience, you take
more responsibility for your own life. Most of all, enjoying
yourself fully in solitude depends on your ability to satisfy
your needs for intimacy with others.

## CRAVINGS FOR INTIMACY

It is hard to be alone when you feel a strong craving to be
with others, to make contact with a special person, to feel
part of a loving support group. According to developmental
theorist Erik Erikson, each person must resolve the struggles between intimacy and isolation, between duty to self
and obligation to others. After having established a healthy
sense of trust during infancy, autonomy and competence
during childhood, and personal identity during adolescence, most people are able by their late teens and early
twenties to bond successfully with others.

Those who are unable to get outside themselves, who
can't risk getting close to others, retreat inside a solitary

shell or occupy themselves in destructive private behavior. They have been unable to establish boundaries that permit closeness without losing themselves in the process. They find it difficult to trust others and lack internal strength to protect themselves from rejection. Over time, they have convinced themselves that they don't need other people around in order to feel content.

Ironically, people who truly enjoy being alone are often those who feel most satisfied with their relationships; those who are uncomfortable in their own company find it difficult to examine the quality and quantity of their human contacts. Enjoying solitude often requires a degree of self-honesty, including a frank assessment of the trust, acceptance, and intimacy you experience.

The fact is that most relationships are fairly superficial and most interactions are all too predictable. Conversations at social gatherings usually cover safe topics—politics, sports, children, vacation plans, movies, books, mutual acquaintances, world events. You recite the stories and jokes you've told a dozen times and listen to others do the same. Rarely are the barriers to true intimacy breached with explorations into more risky areas: "How do you *really* feel about me? What have you always wanted to tell me? When this conversation is over, what are you going to wish you had said?"

You probably have your own favorite ideas of what you would most like to know from the people you are intimate with. The point is that we all long for deeper levels of closeness to others, a contact that can only evolve from greater frankness and openness. In avoiding true intimacy in your relationships, you experience greater loneliness and discomfort in your solitude. Connection to others helps provide the security from which you can feel more connected to yourself. It feels safer to be alone when you know you have the option to be with others you love. That is why satisfying your longings for intimacy makes it so much easier to enjoy your time alone.

The unfulfilled need for intimacy can make reflective time feel empty and frustrating. Take inventory of your relationships: the quality of the time you spend with family, friends, colleagues, neighbors, and acquaintances. Review all the things you say but don't really mean, the lies you tell yourself and almost believe: "It's so good to see you." "You really look great." "No, I'm not bored at all. Do I look bored?" "How am I doing? Oh, just fine. Thanks for asking." "Sure, I'd love to get together some time. Why don't I give you a call?"

Many of us choose to practice a profession that gives us an excuse to stay in contact with others and thereby avoid feeling isolated. In so doing, we are able to be in charge, to maintain control, and protect ourselves from being hurt too easily. The service professions permit us to avoid any real intimacy in relationships by interacting in ritualized, structured ways. For example, in the practice of law, medicine, social work, psychology, counseling, and the clergy, many rules safeguard the participants from getting hurt. In psychotherapy the client may hide behind his defenses for protection against perceived threats, but the professional can hide as well behind a desk, diplomas, and an attitude of objectivity and detachment. Yet, when the client walks out of the office, the helper is once again left alone—to struggle with his or her own fears of intimacy and solitude.

It doesn't work very well, or for very long, to immerse yourself in "safe" relationships. The craving for intimacy remains unsatiated, creating a solitary greenhouse in the mind for cultivating dangerous thoughts and feelings— of self-destruction, of indifference, of hopelessness and frustration.

Private moments can be dangerous not only for the mind but also for the body. Those who live alone, especially not by choice, die younger than those who have companionship; that is true even if the "roommate" is a pet. The lonely are more prone to mental illness, drug abuse, coronary disease, car accidents, hypertension, cancer, and pneumonia. They have a higher frequency of headaches, insomnia, and eating disorders. They are more likely to be murdered and more inclined to kill themselves. While experts are at a loss to explain why intimacy, or at least cohabitation, seems to provide an immunity to certain diseases, it appears as if solitary living, and the loneliness it sometimes fosters, produce additional life stress.

In his investigations of the physical effects of excessive time alone, James Lynch found that the body suffers the consequences of a problem that the mind has ignored. Illness becomes a way for the isolated to seek attention. They are able to elicit sympathy from others and create an excuse for seeking the comfort of their doctor. Every physician's practice is filled with patients who come more for human understanding and caring then they do for medical intervention.

The search for intimacy with others, and for peace in solitude, are the primary motivators in human existence. When you are unsuccessful at meeting these crucial needs, when you feel unfulfilled in your relationships or unhappy in your aloneness, you seek ways to escape your private moments. Only by working to improve both the intimacy of your relationships and the quality of your private moments can you ever hope to reach a point where you feel comfortable with yourself.

## BEING ALONE AND YET WITH OTHERS

Many Eastern as well as Native American cultures do not make the clear demarcation between self and others that has been so important to us in the West. As such, loneliness and alienation are relatively unknown in these cultures. In their view, we are all connected to one another and in harmony with the world of nature.

This counterpoint to self-centeredness is especially important to make in this closing chapter since so much of our discussion throughout the book has been on *individual* needs, *private* moments, *personal* experiences. This, of course, neglects the reality that we all live in a cooperative community of others no matter how isolated we feel. While our search for solitude and individuality is certainly crucial, both for ourselves and society at large, it is equally important that we function effectively as part of a larger whole that includes family, social circles, professional affiliations, and Nature.

From the earliest philosophers and Confucian scholars, from the Romantic poets of Wordsworth's era, to the present-day transpersonal psychologists, there has always been a voice that speaks of the unity of all living things. It is indeed possible to stand alone, as an individual reveling in freedom and privacy, without experiencing estrangement from others. This is accomplished in several ways:

*Through an appreciation and tolerance of individual differences.* It is one thing to discover what is best for yourself, whether it is old-time religion or rock and roll; it is quite another to allow others to find their own paths to contentment in ways that are strikingly different from your own, and to do so without critical judgment. Differences, conflicts, arguments, and wars arise when one group attempts to impose its will on others. It is not necessary to recruit anyone else to your point of view in order to enjoy your chosen path.

*Through a gentleness of spirit.* While it does require considerable strength and fortitude to stand up for what you know is best, it also takes great patience, sensitivity, and diplomacy to meet your private needs without unduly alienating or offending those you love most.

*Through compromise.* When you get what you want, the significant others in your life often feel it is at their expense. For this reason, negotiation and compromise are necessary. This often occurs among couples in which one partner has decided that she or he wants more freedom and private space and the other partner feels extremely threatened. The marital relationship was established under one set of rules (with regard to household chores, for example), and then abruptly one spouse decides another arrangement might be more equitable. If both spouses are willing to hear the other's point of view, if they can both stay open and flexible, it is likely they will eventually reach a compromise acceptable to both—one that is fair to both partners and one that gives them both time to adjust to the new set of rules.

*Through commitment to the community.*   A balance between private and public moments is necessary in order to create a satisfying life. In *Habits of the Heart*, sociologist Robert Bellah and his colleagues explore the reconciliation of the polarities of individualism versus community commitment. They point out that the "quest for purely private fulfillment is illusory; it often ends in emptiness instead." Bellah's group, which has studied intimately the private and public lives of hundreds of people, concludes that the two need not be at odds. Public and private selves are two halves of a whole. They are not in competition with each other but, in the words of Parker Palmer in *The Company of Strangers*, "They work together dialectically, helping to create and nurture one another."

## SERVING TWO MASTERS: INDIVIDUAL AND COMMUNITY DEMANDS

While in theory it is possible that the demands of society and your own internal needs can be reconciled, in practice this task is the greatest challenge of modern life. The bind we find ourselves in goes something like this:

*Option 1:* Act according to the values, expectations, and norms established for you by external authorities, including religious, civic, legislative, legal, and moral bodies.

*Result:* While you will win the respect, admiration, and approval of friends, colleagues, and society at large, it is often at the expense of personal desires. The result is often feelings of stress and frustration from stifling natural impulses. While you are doing the "right" thing, you may not feel so good about other things you are missing.

*Option 2:* Act according to your individual urges and internal drives, and consistent with your own code of conduct. Indulge your secret self, living out the activities and behaviors that are important to you but may be disapproved of by others.

*Result:* You feel a surge of gratification in realizing your own potential and living up to your personal standards, as well as tremendous satisfaction in recognizing and meeting your own needs. However, the consequence of indulging your secret self is often the development of guilt, shame, and remorse. You have the generalized feeling that you have been "bad" and somehow let others down.

*Option 3:* The paradox is that in order to serve society, you have to take care of yourself. But if your self-nurturance involves things that society would not sanction, the only healthy alternative is to do them in private and *feel good about yourself in the process.* This is no easy task, for it requires a high degree of self-esteem to give yourself permission to be yourself and to suspend all internal criticisms as well as remaining immune to external pressures. Remember that societal norms have been established to force compliance, stifle individual differences to avoid deviance, and preserve the stability of the community. It is therefore possible to become a model of responsible citizenship as far as others are concerned, and yet honor in private those unique parts of you that are productive, pleasurable, and self-enhancing.

Philosopher Alan Watts makes the interesting point that aloneness is an illusion, "that the world beyond the skin is actually an extension of our bodies." According to this Eastern view, we can never be alone as long as we feel connected to others, bonded to something bigger than ourselves—whether that is a personal God, a spiritual grounding to the Earth, or a commitment to loving and helping others.

I spoke earlier of the terror we experience in confronting our own mortality, the isolation of being locked into a membrane that separates our essential self from others. Watts offers some comfort: "This feeling of being lonely and very temporary visitors in the universe is in flat contradiction to everything known about man (and all other living organisms) in the sciences. We do not 'come into' this world; we come *out* of it, as leaves from a tree."

It is this feeling of interconnectedness to the planet, to all its inhabitants, that allows us to celebrate our private moments and secret selves. We have the knowledge that no matter what we do when we're alone or how we feel about it, others are doing pretty much the same thing. Everyone experiences the terror of abandonment, the despair of loneliness, the fear of rejection. At times, alienation and isolation are familiar company. We all have strange thoughts and do unusual things when nobody is looking, things that we will never share with anyone.

Regardless of your present state of functioning as a solitary being—whether you are already quite skilled at enjoying your solitude, or whether you wish to reduce negative feelings about being in your own company—you can enrich the quality of your private moments. You were born into the world alone, and alone you will exit it. How satisfying your life feels in between these two points depends very much on your willingness to pursue the themes discussed in this book: to appreciate better your inner world, to become more self-directed, to be more self-nurturing and playful, to counteract resistance and obstacles you encounter, and to face yourself without distractions.

With dedication and commitment to developing the art of being alone, you will become even more able to increase your independence, productivity, creativity, enjoyment of the spontaneous private moments that make up a significant part of your life. As you become more and more proficient at taking care of yourself and meeting your own needs, you increase your capacity for taking care of and loving others.

# Bibliography

Adler, M. *Ten Philosophical Mistakes.* New York: Collier, 1985.

Ardry, R. *The Territorial Imperative.* New York: Dell, 1966.

Aries, P. *Centuries of Childhood.* New York: Vintage Books, 1960.

Artzybasheff, M. *The Breaking Point.* New York: B. W. Heubsch, 1917.

Audy, J. R. "Man the Lonely Animal: Biological Roots of Loneliness." In *The Anatomy of Loneliness,* edited by Hartog, Audy, and Cohen. New York: International University Press, 1980.

Baudelaire, C. *My Heart Laid Bare,* quoted in *Solitude in Society,* by R. Sayre. Cambridge, Mass.: Harvard University Press, 1978.

Beck, A. T. *Cognitive Therapy and the Emotional Disorders.* New York: International University Press, 1976.

Bellah, R. N.; Madsen, R.; Sullivan, W. M.; Swidler, A.; and Tipton, S. M. *Habits of the Heart: Individualism and Commitment in American Life.* New York: Harper & Row, 1985.

Bensman, J., and Lilienfeld, R. *Between Public and Private: The Lost Boundaries of Self.* New York: The Free Press, 1979.

Berdaeyev, N. *Solitude and Society.* London: Centenary Press, 1947.

Bernikow, L. *Alone in America.* New York: Harper & Row, 1978.

Bigbee, H. "Loneliness, Solitude, and the Twofold Way in Which Concern Seems to Be Claimed." *Humanitas* 10 (3), 1974, 313.

Borger, I. "Privacy." Unpublished essay.

Breuer, G. *Sociobiology and the Human Dimension.* Cambridge, England: Cambridge University Press, 1982.

Bugental, J. F. T. *The Search for Existential Identity.* San Francisco: Jossey-Bass, 1976.

Byrd, R. *Alone.* Los Angeles: Jeremy P. Tarcher, 1938.

Byrnes, D. A. "Life Skills in Solitude and Silence in the School." *Education* 104 (1), 1983.

Calhoun, J. B. "Seven Steps from Loneliness." In *The Anatomy of Loneliness,* edited by Hartog, Audy, and Cohen. New York: International University Press, 1980.

Campbell, J. *Myths to Live By.* New York: Bantam, 1973.

Camus, A. *The Outsider.* New York: Penguin Books, 1961.

_____ . *Notebooks 1935–1942.* New York: Harcourt Brace Jovanovich, 1963.

Carkhuff, R. *The Art of Problem Solving.* Amherst, Mass.: HRD Press, 1973.

Clough, W. O. *The Necessary Earth: Nature and Solitude in American Literature.* Austin: University of Texas Press, 1964.

Cohen, J. M., and Phipps, J. F. *The Common Experience.* Los Angeles: Jeremy P. Tarcher, 1979.

Csikszentmihalyi, M. *Beyond Boredom and Anxiety.* San Francisco: Jossey-Bass, 1975.

Csikszentmihalyi, M., and Larson, R. *Being Adolescent.* New York: Basic Books, 1984.

Deaton, J. E.; Berg, S. W.; and Richlin, M. "Coping Activities in Solitary Confinement of U.S. Navy POW's in Vietnam." *Journal of Applied Social Psychology* 7 (3), 1977.

Ellis, A. *Humanistic Psychotherapy.* New York: Julian Press, 1973.

_____ . "Forward." In *Human Autoerotic Practices,* edited by M. F. DeMartino. New York: Human Sciences, 1979.

Falbo, T. *The Single-Child Family.* New York: Guilford Press, 1984.

Farb, P. *Humankind.* New York: Bantam, 1980.

Frankl, V. *Man's Search for Meaning.* New York: Washington Square Press, 1963.

Freud, S. "Obsessive Actions and Religious Beliefs." In *The Standard Edition of the Complete Psychological Works of Sigmund Freud,* Vol. 9 (1906–1908), edited by J. Strachey. London: Hogarth Press, 1958.

Freyberg, J. T. "Hold high the Cardboard Sword." *Psychology Today,* Feb. 1975, 63–64.

Fuchs, V. R. *Who Shall Live?* New York: Basic Books, 1974.

Gotesky, R. "Aloneness, Loneliness, Isolation, and Solitude." In *An Invitation to Phenomenology,* edited by J. M. Edie. Chicago: Quadrangle, 1965.

Hall, E. T. *The Hidden Dimension.* Garden City, N.Y.: Anchor Books, 1969.

Hammitt, W. E., "Cognitive Dimensions of Wilderness Solitude." *Environment and Behavior* 14 (4), 1982.

Harris, M. *Cannibals and Kings: The Origins of Cultures.* New York: Vintage Books, 1977.

Hathaway, B. "Running to Run." *Psychology Today,* July 1984.

Healy, S. D. *Boredom, Self, and Culture.* London: Associated University Press, 1984.

Hobson, R. *Forms of Feeling.* London: Tavistock Publications, 1985.

Hosner, M. "A Life Apart." Masters thesis, Center for Humanistic Studies, Detroit, 1987.

Howard, J. A. *The Flesh-Colored Cage.* New York: Hawthorn, 1975.

Hulme, W. E. *Creative Loneliness.* Minneapolis: Augsburg Publishing, 1977.

Humphrey, N. *Meditation: The Inner Way.* Wellingborough, England: The Aquarian Press, 1987.

Huxley, A. *The Doors of Perception.* New York: Harper & Row, 1954.

Keen, S. "Boredom and How to Beat It." *Psychology Today,* May 1977, 80.

Kelsey, M. *Transcend: A Guide to the Spiritual Quest.* New York: Crossroad Publishing, 1981.

Kersten, F. "Loneliness and Solitude." *Humanitas* 10 (3), 1974.

Kierkegaard, S. *Either/Or.* Princeton, N.J.: Princeton University Press, 1944.

———. *Sickness Unto Death.* Garden City, N.Y.: Doubleday, 1954.

Klinger, E. "The Power of Daydreams." *Psychology Today,* Oct. 1987.

———. *Daydreaming: Your Hidden Resource for Self-Knowledge and Creativity.* Los Angeles: Jeremy P. Tarcher, 1990.

Koestler, A. *The Act of Creation.* London: Macmillan, 1969.

Kora, T., and Ohara, K. "Morita Therapy." *Psychology Today* 6 (10), 1973.

Kottler, J. A. *On Being a Therapist.* San Francisco: Jossey-Bass, 1986.

Kubey, R. W. "Television: Idle Comfort," reported in *Psychology Today* by J. Goetz, June 1987.

Kubistant, T. "Resolutions of Aloneliness." *Personnel and Guidance Journal,* March 1981.

Landau, J. "Loneliness and Creativity." In *The Anatomy of Loneliness,* edited by Hartog, Audy, and Cohen. New York: International University Press, 1980.

Larson, R., and Csikszentmihalyi, M. "Experimental Correlates of Time Alone in Adolescence." *Journal of Personality* 46 (4), 1978.

Larson, R.; Csikszentmihalyi, M.; and Graef, R. "Time Alone in Daily Experience: Loneliness or Renewal?" In *Loneliness: A Sourcebook of Current Theory, Research, and Therapy,* edited by L. Peplau and D. Perlman. New York: Wiley, 1982.

Larson, R., and Johnson, C. "Bulimia: Disturbed Patterns of Solitude." *Addictive Behavior* 10, 1985.

de Laubier, P. "Sociological Aspects of Solitude in Advanced Industrial Societies." *Labour and Society* 9 (1), 1984.

Lear, M. "The Pain of Loneliness." *The New York Times Magazine,* Dec. 20, 1987.

Lopata, H. Z. "Loneliness: Forms and Components." *Social Problems* 17, 1969.

Lorenz, K. *Evolution and the Modification of Behavior.* Chicago: University of Chicago Press, 1965.

Lubin, A. *Stranger on the Earth: The Life of Vincent Van Gogh.* New York: Holt, Rinehart, and Winston, 1972.

Lynch, J. J. *The Broken Heart: The Medical Consequences of Loneliness.* New York: Basic Books, 1977.

Marcus, I. M., and Francis, J. J. *Masturbation: From Infancy to Senescence.* New York: International Universities Press, 1975.

Marsh, P., and Collett, P. *Driving Passion: The Psychology of the Car.* Boston: Faber and Faber, 1989.

Marshall, M. "Solitude." Masters thesis, Center for Humanistic Studies, Detroit, 1985.

Maslow, A. *Toward a Psychology of Being.* New York: A. Van Nostrand, 1968.

May, R. *The Courage to Create.* New York: W. W. Norton, 1975.

Merton, T. *The Monastic Journey.* Kansas City: Andrews and McMeel, 1977.

———. *Love and Learning.* New York: Farrar, Straus Giroux, 1979.

Mijuskovic, B. "Types of Loneliness." *Psychology* 14, 1977.

Miller, H. *Tropic of Cancer.* New York: Grove Press, 1961.

———. *Henry Miller on Writing.* New York: New Directions, 1964.

Montagu, A. *Touching.* New York: Harper & Row, 1978.

Montaigne, M. *The Complete Essays of Montaigne.* Stanford, Calif.: Stanford University Press, 1965.

Moore, B. *Privacy: Studies in Social and Cultural History.* Armonk, N.Y.: M. E. Sharpe, 1984.

Morgan, O. J. "Music for the Dance: Some Meanings of Solitude." *Journal of Religion and Health* 25 (1), 1986, 24.

Morris, D. *Manwatching: A Field Guide to Human Behavior.* New York: Harry Abrams, 1977.

Morris, S., and Charney, N. "Insomnia: Don't Lose Sleep Over It." *Psychology Today,* April 1983, 82.

Moss, R. *The I That Is We.* Berkeley, Calif.: Celestial Arts, 1981.

Mosse, E. *The Conquest of Loneliness.* New York: Random House, 1967.

Moustakas, C. *Loneliness.* New York: Prentice-Hall, 1961.

_____ . *Loneliness and Love.* Englewood Cliffs, N.J.: Prentice-Hall, 1972, 20.

Neale, R. E. *Loneliness, Solitude, and Companionship.* Philadelphia: Westminister Press, 1984.

Neale, T. *An Island to Myself.* London: Collins Publishers, 1966.

Nin, A. "Preface." In *The New Diary,* by T. Rainer. Los Angeles: J. P. Tarcher, 1978.

Nisenbaum, S. "Ways of Being Alone in the World." *American Behavioral Scientist* 27 (6), 1984.

Ornstein, R. E. *The Psychology of Consciousness.* New York: Harcourt, Brace, Jovanovich, 1977.

Palmer, P. J. *The Company of Strangers.* New York: Crossroad, 1981.

Pascal, B. *Pensées.* Baltimore: Penguin, 1966.

Pedersen, D. M. "Personality Correlates of Privacy." *Journal of Psychology* 112, 1982.

Rahner, K. "Thoughts on the Theology of Christmas." *Theological Investigations*, Vol. 3. New York: Seabury Press, 1974.

Rainer, T. *The New Diary.* Los Angeles: Jeremy P. Tarcher, 1978.

Rapoport, J. *The Boy Who Couldn't Stop Washing.* New York: E. P. Dutton, 1989.

Reynolds, D. K. *Morita Psychotherapy.* Berkeley: University of California Press, 1976.

Rilke, R. M. *The Notebooks of Malte Laurids Brigge.* New York: W. W. Norton, 1949.

Rosenbaum, J., and Rosenbaum, V. *Conquering Loneliness.* New York: Hawthorne Books, 1973.

Rousseau, J. J. *Reveries of a Solitary Walker.* New York: Penguin Books, 1979.

Roth, P. *Portnoy's Complaint.* New York: Random House, 1969.

Rubinstein, C., and Shaver, P. "The Experience of Loneliness." In *Loneliness: A Sourcebook of Current Theory, Research, and Therapy,* edited by Peplau and Perlman. New York: Wiley, 1982.

Rubinstein, C.; Shaver, P.; and Peplau, L. A. "Loneliness." *Human Nature,* Feb. 1979.

Russell, B. *The Autobiography of Bertrand Russell.* London: Allen Unwin, 1967.

Russell, D.; Peplau, L. A.; and Ferguson, M. L. "Developing a Measure of Loneliness." *Journal of Personality Assessment* 42, 1978.

Russianoff, P. *Why Do I Think I Am Nothing Without a Man?* New York: Bantam, 1982.

Rutledge, H. A. *In the Presence of Mine Enemies.* Old Tappen, N.J.: Fleming H. Revell, 1973.

Sadler, W. A., and Johnson, T. B. "From Loneliness to Anomia." In *The Anatomy of Loneliness,* edited by Hartog, Audy, and Cohen. New York: International University Press, 1980.

Sarton, M. *Journal of a Solitude.* New York: W. W. Norton, 1973.

Schneider, C. D. *Shame, Exposure, and Privacy.* Boston: Beacon Press, 1977.

Schwartz, B. "The Social Psychology of Privacy." *American Journal of Sociology* 73 (6), 1968.

Scott-Maxwell, F. *The Measure of My Days.* New York: Alfred A. Knopf, 1973.

Shneidman, E. "At the Point of No Return." *Psychology Today,* March 1987.

Singer, J. *Daydreaming and Fantasy.* Oxford, England: Oxford University Press, 1981.

———— . "Fantasy: the Foundation of Serenity." *Psychology Today,* Oct. 1987.

Slater, P. *The Pursuit of Loneliness.* Boston: Beacon Press, 1976.

Slocum, J. *Sailing Alone Around the World.* New York: Collier-Macmillan, 1970.

Smith, A. *Powers of Mind.* New York: Random House, 1975.

Solomon, J. *The Signs of Our Time.* Los Angeles: Jeremy P. Tarcher, 1988.

Steinbeck, J. *Journal of a Novel.* New York: Bantam, 1969.

Storr, A. *Solitude: A Return to the Self.* New York: The Free Press, 1988.

Suedfeld, P. *Restricted Environmental Stimulation.* New York: Wiley, 1980.

Tanner, I. *Loneliness: The Fear of Love.* New York: Harper & Row, 1973.

Thoreau, H. D. *Walden.* New York: Lancer Books, 1968.

Tillich, P. *The Eternal Now.* New York: Scribners, 1963.

Timmerman, J. *Prisoner Without a Name, Cell Without a Number.* New York: Vintage Books, 1981.

Turkle, S. *The Second Self.* New York: Simon and Schuster, 1984.

Watts, A. *The Book: On the Taboo Against Knowing Who You Are.* New York: Vintage, 1972.

Webster, C. D.; Konstantareas, M. M.; Oxman, J.; and Mack, J., eds. *Autism.* New York: Pergamon Press, 1980.

Weil, A. *The Natural Mind.* Boston: Houghton Mifflin, 1972.

———— . *Health and Healing.* Boston: Houghton Mifflin, 1983.

Westin, A. *Privacy and Freedom.* New York: Atheneum, 1967.

Williams, T. *Memoirs.* New York: Doubleday, 1976.

Wolfe, T. *Look Homeward Angel.* New York: Scribners, 1929.

———— . *The Hills Beyond.* New York: Harper & Row, 1941.

Yalom, I. *Existential Psychotherapy.* New York: Basic Books, 1980.

Young, J. "Loneliness, Depression, and Cognitive Therapy: Theory and Application." In *Loneliness: A Sourcebook of Current Theory, Research, and Therapy,* edited by Peplau and Perlman. New York: Wiley, 1982.

Zimbardo, P. *Shyness.* Reading, Mass.: Addison-Wesley, 1977.